Buff Orpington Chickens
as Pets

Buff Orpington Chickens Owner's Manual

by

Roland Ruthersdale

Contents

Table of Contents

Table of Contents

Introduction

Without the slightest doubt, chickens are wonderful pets to have. They have a very quirky personality and they can be quite entertaining when they are kept as backyard pets. The thing about chickens is that they are rather different from the regular pets that one would have at home.

You see, with pets like dogs and cats, it is possible to get a lot of support and feedback from other owners. With chickens, the number of owners are fewer and therefore, the information that you can rely upon is a lot less. Since keeping chickens as pets is growing to be very popular in the urban set up, you might be tempted to bring home a little flock of your own and raise them to be loving companions.

The most important thing that you must understand with chickens is that keeping them requires a great deal of commitment and responsibility. Most new owners think that as long as the chicken has a big flock to scurry around with and also has some food to munch on, they have got what it takes to have a chicken as a pet. However, that is quite the contrary. Although chickens seem to be busy in a world of their own, they are extremely emotional creatures who can get highly attached to their owners. Therefore, having chickens as pets is not just a physical or financial responsibility; it is a very emotional one. Chickens are really dependant on their owners for some love and attention. They need to know that they are being looked after. These birds are also extremely susceptible to stress. They will be really anxious and extremely affected on an emotional level if they are not happy in the surroundings or the environment that they live in. They are so sensitive that they will even fall sick at the slightest disturbance in their immediate surroundings.

As the owner of any poultry, it is one's responsibility to ensure that they receive all the things that they need on a regular basis. This includes fresh water, clean housing and of course, food. You must create an environment in which you can be assured that your poultry remains safe and healthy. You see, in a flock of birds such as chickens, diseases can be quite rampant. This means that having one bird that is infected will lead to the entire flock getting affected in no time. So their visits to veterinarians and their annual vaccinations are highly important if you want to ensure that they are at the best of their physical well-being.

With all these responsibilities comes a host of advantages of having chickens in your home. To begin with, having chickens is a great way to ensure a good source of nutrition, i.e. the eggs. You will have access to fresh and clean eggs at your doorstep, that too for free. Some people like to keep chickens in their homes as they make great show pets. There are some varieties that come with beautifully colored plumes that you can show off at popular pet and poultry shows. There are some breeds such as the Spanish Andalusian that come with really sleek feathers. Then, there are others that have gorgeous fluffy and silky feathers.

If you are interested in raising chickens for the meat, that is a whole other story. Of course, you want to ensure that the poultry that you are breeding has no chemicals or hormones. This guarantees your family with free range meat that is not processed and is really fresh.

The first thing that you need to do when you bring home chickens is to understand the purpose of having these birds at home. Then you can choose among the different varieties that are available. These birds are divided into three primary categories: Pure bred, hybrids and Buff Orpington Chickens. Pure bred chickens are those that come from a strain or a breed that is widely recognised and accepted. They are bred for generations without any breeding with other strains of chickens. The hybrids are those that come with a mixed lineage. Usually, these birds are bred to retain two desirable traits from different breeds or to eliminate certain undesirable traits from a certain breed. The last category is the Buff Orpington Chicken, a smaller sized chicken. Buff Orpington Chickens can be any breed off chicken but in a size that is almost half that of the regular breed. These chickens are mainly bred to make backyard pets. Since they are petite, they can be kept in the smallest of spaces. They have all the characteristics of the breed that you like but they are smaller and easier to care for.

Irrespective of the type of breed that you bring home, you must be well aware of the responsibility that you are getting into. This book is your complete guide into selecting and taking care of chickens. It will take you through all the common questions that a new chicken owner will have. I hope that this book is of great use to all of you aspiring chicken owners who are dabbling the Internet for answers to your queries.

Chapter 1: The Buff Orpington Chickens

The Buff Orpington Chickens were first made in the mid 19th century in Orpington, Kent. Of course, they derive their name from their place of birth. These chickens have become popular across the chicken breeding community for their dual purpose. These attractive birds have found homes in several Urban Backyards because of their ability to live comfortably amidst their human companions.

Although the Orpington Chicken started out as a utility bird, it gained extreme popularity globally as a great show bird. The fully feathered beauties were known for the varieties of colors that they were available in. Even today, several exhibitors are trying to produce show birds that are desirable and interesting. In fact, there are several varieties that have been developed using different strains of Buff Orpingtons alone!

Sometimes when the existing birds are bred with other native chicken breeds, there are offsprings that closely resemble an entirely different chicken variety altogether. This mixture and out crossing has made it very difficult to identify the exact origin of most Orpington strains. In addition to that, their feathering is so profuse that, most often, you are unable to define the coloring of these beautiful birds.

However, they are the favorites amongst all the newcomers in the world of chicken keeping and breeding as they have all the desirable characteristics of a good chicken breed. They are magnificent birds that are quite large in form. The Buff Orpington variety is, perhaps, the most popular of all the varieties of the Orpington Chickens. They are known to be great show quality birds and are fondly known as "Golden Chickens" by exhibitors.

1. Why are they valuable?

Buff Orpington Chickens make perfect pets. They are extremely calm and docile, making it easy for them to get adapted to the environment that is provided for them. They are also extremely cuddly as their feathers are soft and full. If you are looking for a pet that you can fondle and play with, the Buff Orpington Chicken might be the perfect choice for you. They are also very pleasant birds, seldom getting into fights.

Buff Orpingtons are excellent egg layers. They can lay close to 200 eggs each year. However, they are not the most preferred breeds for an egg business as they are known to be an infertile breed. When they are fertile, they are prolific egg layers. However, because of their sheer size, the Orpingtons find it quite hard to breed and actually fertilize the eggs. So, in each batch of eggs that is laid, the purpose is to hatch as many to get that "Golden Bird" that will shine in exhibitions.

That brings us to the most important quality of the Orpington Birds. They did start off as utility birds but, soon, exhibitors understood the importance of this breed in showing. Several strains of Orpingtons have been created over the years. They have been bred for the color varieties and the quality of their feathering that makes them very popular in the show business.

Of course, the quality of meat is also great with Buff Orpington Chickens. They are valued for their contribution to the meat production industry as well.

2. Characteristics of Buff Orpington Chickens

Here are some standard characteristics that will help you understand if a Buff Orpington Chicken is the pet that you are really looking for. These are generalised traits. However, depending upon whether you get miniatures of standard breeds or true Buff Orpington Chickens, there are specific traits that you must look out for.

Size and Shape: Buff Orpington Chickens have a massive structure. They are usually prized for their size. Their bodies are usually broad and deep. The outline of a Buff Orpington Chicken is rather interesting as the curved back gives it a distinct concave shape.

They usually have a short tail. The rump or the cushion is wide but has a distinct flat structure.

Comb, Wattles and Earlobes: Buff Orpingtons usually have a single comb with five properly defined points. They stand upright in the males. The size of the comb is medium. The bright red color stands out against their dark and light plumes. The wattles are also medium sized. The wattles and the earlobes are bright red in color.

Broodiness: Orpington Chickens are great mothers. They will get broody when they are able to lay eggs. The only drawback of this breed is that their egg laying abilities are great only as long as the bird is fertile. Because of the massive size of their bodies, these birds tend to find it hard to make and lay eggs every season.

Colors: The coloration of the various parts of the bird is different as per the color of the bird. The dark and light varieties exhibit strikingly different color patterns.

White Orpington:

- Beak: White
- Legs and Feet: White

- Earlobes: Bright Red
- Eyes: Red
- Comb: Bright Red
- Wattle: Bright Red

Dark Orpingtons
- Beak: Black
- Legs and Feet: Black or Blue
- Earlobes: Bright Red
- Eyes: Dark brown or black
- Comb: Bright Red
- Wattle: Bright Red
- Toenails: White

Carriage

According to the standards described for Buff Orpingtons, they should have a carriage that is bold and upright. Basically, the birds should have a carriage that makes them look active. Of course, the standards prescribed have been often debated as the upright posture only applies to birds that are tall. The modern Buff Orpingtons, on the other hand, are rounded birds. In addition to that, with the profuse feathering that is preferred by most breeders, the gait is not really graceful. These birds tend to bounce along when they walk instead of gliding as expected.

Plumage

There are several color options available with the Orpington chickens as you known by now. There is one characteristic of the plumage that is common for all varieties. It is expected that the plumage is close and not very fluffy and loose. The plumage should also be soft and not hard like most breeds.

As for the dark varieties of birds, it is permitted for them to have a sort of green sheen to their plumes. However, if there is a purple sheen, it is not accepted for showing. The most interesting of all the types of Orpingtons are the Buff Orpingtons. These birds are light brown or golden in color. They may have browning in their tails sometimes. However, white flecks and pale coloring is not accepted. These birds cannot have any other feathering besides buff throughout the body. They cannot have any black or white coloration in their plumes. Of course, their skin is always white.

3. Different Varieties and Parentage

There are several breeds or varieties of Orpington Chickens that are available. Although the Buff Orpington breed is most popular, there are other varieties that have been experimented with on a regular basis. The parentage of these birds depends upon the coloration of the feathers. Here are some popular varieties of Orpingtons:

Type	Parentage
Black	The original Orpington variety that was developed by out crossing a Black Minorca cock and a Black Plymoth variety. The female that was the result of this mating was crossed with a black Langshan to create the Black Orpington.
White	A white leghorn was crossed with a black hamburgh. The white pullets that resulted from this cross were then bred with a White Dorking Cock to create the White Orpington
Buff	A Gold Spangled Hamburgh was mated with a Dorking and the resulting pullets were then mated with a Buff Cochin Cock
Jubilee	They were created from Dark Orpingtons, Gold Spangled Hamburgs and Red Dorkings
Spangled	These birds were the result of an outcross between a Jubilee and a Black Orpington

Cuckoo	These birds were the result of an outcross between a White and Black Orpington
Blue	They were again the result of an outcross between a White and Black Orpington
Red	They were selected from a batch of Dark Buff Orpingtons

Now that you know everything that you need to know about the characteristics of the Buff Orpington Chickens, you should be able to select the perfect one for your home. For those who are interested in showing these magnificent birds, you will be able to retain all the desirable qualities of these massive chickens.

The next chapter talks about the fascinating history of the Orpington Chickens. This is the journey of this breed from being an ordinary utility bird to becoming the most preferred show and exhibition bird.

Chapter 2: History of Buff Orpington Chickens

Orpington Chickens were developed by William Cook from Orpington, Kent in the year 1886. The first bird that was created was black in color and was introduced as a dual purpose domestic fowl. These birds were supposed to be reared for their meat and their eggs. However, they became best suited for exhibiting as their strain was extremely versatile and was capable of being molded into various colors and shapes as desired by the exhibitors. These birds were exhibited for the first time in the London Dairy show in the year 1886.

A year later a club was formed to promote and develop the new breed. It was originally called the Orpington Club and was later named the Black Orpington Club. Experiments with different strains resulted in the creation of the White Orpington in the year 1889. Then, following the success of his Black Orpington, William Cook experimented with the breed to create the Buff Orpington Chicken in the year 1894.

The Buff Orpington Chicken rose to fame pretty quickly. In fact, in just four years, the Buff Orpington Club was formed in

England. Since the breed was gaining a lot of popularity in England, a special version was created to commemorate the Diamond Jubilee Celebrations of Queen Victoria. This breed was named the Jubilee Orpington.

It was after the creation of the buff variety that the Orpington breed gained a lot of popularity. These birds became the ideal multi-purpose chickens. Not only were they great for exhibitions, they were also very well known for their broodiness.

Between the early and mid 20th century, the Buff Orpington Chicken was the most preferred breed for brooding in most farms. Even today, these birds are considered to be great brooders by hobbyists.

They were first introduced in America in the year 1890 at the Massachusetts Poultry Association Show that was held in Boston. This is when the Single Comb Black Orpingtons were exhibited at the show. After 9 years, the Single Comb Buff Orpington was displayed at the Madison Square Garden Show in New York.

Although it took the Americans some time to grow fond of this English Chicken breed, by 1901 these birds had become quite a rage in the country. The entries to the Madison Square Garden Show increased to nineteen single Buff Orpingtons. Until then, they were considered a market handicap as they did not have the standard yellow leg and skin that was preferred in the American Market.

After that, the Orpingtons became popular even in other parts of the world. In fact, new breeds like the Australorp were developed in Australia. Although this bird was recognized as a unique breed, it was derived from the Black Orpington. These birds were exported to the UK in 1921 as Utility Black Orpingtons. This was done almost 34 years after the first Orpington Chicken came to Australia.

Today, Orpingtons are bred for several reasons. Mostly, they are preferred by hobbyists who are trying to make a name in the world of showing and exhibiting chickens.

Chapter 3: Summary of Buff Orpington Chicken Traits

Size: Large or Heavy weighing about 4 to 5 kgs or 8 to 10 lbs

Varieties Recognised: Buff , Black, White, Blue and Jubilee

Occurrence: Common

Purpose: Domestic, Commercial and Show

Temperament: Active yet docile. Roosters can be aggressive

Hardiness: Can manage heat and cold. Very hardy breed. The comb is vulnerable to frostbites

Egg Production: 5 eggs each week

Color of the egg: Pale Brown

Size of the egg: Large

Comb: Single or rose

Feathered Legs: No

These are just a few characteristics that are unique to the Buff Orpington Chickens. However, the breed standards have been discussed in detail in the previous chapters.

Chapter 4: History of Domesticating Chickens

The history of domesticating chickens is rather interesting. The biggest mystery till date is what came first? The chicken or the egg? As debatable as this subject is, research shows that even the world of science does not have an answer for this.

Some scientists believe that as dinosaurs evolved into birds, chicken eggs were formed. The eggs that belonged to the reptiles then are the predecessors of the modern chicken egg. So, one part of the world of science holds that the chicken egg came first.

Another section of the world of science believes that chickens did come first after all as they found a common protein in the eggs and the chickens. But either way, the evidence suggests that chickens as we know them today, developed from the Red Jungle fowl breed which was found in the forests of India and Thailand. They then developed into several breeds as they were carried from one country to another.

Chickens were a very popular form of domesticated poultry even back then. Evidence actually suggests that the Roman Empire used to breed chickens. There are several paintings that were found in on pottery and also on the walls of the Roman times. Before people started consuming the meat, these birds were used exclusively as sacrifice for the gods.

The Romans believed that by slaughtering the chickens, they would be able to make better decisions in the battlefield. In fact, there was a special position in the Roman army called the "Keeper of the Sacred Chickens." The sacrificial birds were carried in a cage whenever a King went to war.

When the army was under attack, a few crumbs of bread would be thrown into these cages. If the chickens decided to eat the food, then it meant that all would be well. On the other hand, when the chickens did not eat, it was a sign that they should be cautious in every move that they make during the war.

There is a popular Roman legend about a war in which the chickens refused to eat the food that was put into the cage. The general of that Roman army, Publius Claudius Pulcher ignored this omen and threw the cage into the sea saying that the birds could drink if they refused to eat. This was the battle of Drepanum that the Romans lost quite terribly.

The Greeks had a different approach. When they wanted to appease their Gods, they would offer chickens. They believed that they would get what they wanted if they did this.

The next question is how these birds got half the world around to America. According to historical records, Christopher Columbus is responsible for this. When he voyaged from Italy to the new World, he carried these birds in the ships.

With the advantage of technology, scientists today are conducting several DNA tests on the chickens to find more specific answers. To understand how chickens got to America, they are trying to study the bones of chickens that were found in North and South America. According to the research, these bones are much older than era in which Columbus made his way to America. This indicates a possibility of another breed of chicken that was developed there from some other breed of bird. They also believe that an explorer before Columbus brought these birds there.

Between the 16th and 20th centuries, chickens became very popular among small farms. They were even raised in family backyards for the eggs that they produced. It was only in 1923 that the poultry industry in America boomed. It was the result of a housewife named Cecilia Steele from the Sussex County. She was the one who suggested that chicken could also be sold as a broiler only for the meat. While all along the chickens were only raised as layers, this suggestion revolutionised the industry.

When she saw potential in the broiler variety, she purchased 500 chickens. She decided to sell them only for meat. At that time poultry was not a common choice for meat. It was a delicacy. So the first lot fetched her about 62 cents per pound. By 1924, she was able to sell her stock for 57 cents per pound. That is equivalent to about $15 per pound today.

People realised how versatile the chicken meat was. They could boil, stew, fry and roast the meat. This increased the demand for chicken meat. In less than two years, the flock that Steele owned increased to 10,000. Ten years later, she was the owner of seven farms.

Even to this day, Delaware, which is the birthplace of the broiler chicken, is the largest producer of this variety. They deliver millions of chickens each year.

1. Industrialization of domesticating chickens

For a really long time, the domestication of chickens was restricted to small farm owners. In the 1940s, it became a full-fledged industry. Before this, all the small farms and mills worked as per guidelines set by the National Chicken Council. When these small units integrated, the industry became more streamlined.

It became a well-coordinated industry. The feed mills promoted the farms by loaning them money to buy the chickens. These farmers in turn sold the meat to the processors. The money that they got from this sale was used to repay the feed mill that sponsored them. This system became more and more efficient with the increase in demand.

Another important factor that promoted the industry was the introduction of the process of refrigeration. With this technology, it was possible to store the meat for longer. The advantage of producing meat and eggs in factories was that they were able to produce more with less investment. The whole process of raising the chicken became an issue with the smaller farmers as it was pretty difficult.

By the 1950s, an event called the Baby Boom occurred. This made it mandatory to increase the production by and large. During this period, most people opted for the vertical integration model which meant that one company had complete control over the marketing and production. This effort was taken to make the industry more cost effective. The new companies were able to afford machinery and technology.

By this time, it was the entrepreneurs who used the vertical integration model who had complete control over the industry. During the 1960s, promotion of the chicken industry was extended to print and television. This is when several brands were born and actually recognised by the common people.

By now, the industry had become so popular that automation was a must. They had to make use of technology that would cut down on the labor and the time consumed in the process.

It was in the 1970s that automation was actually introduced to meet the demands of the consumers. There were stricter laws and regulations to govern this industry. Most of the laws were focused on creating better products. People, too, were better informed about the nutritional value of the meat and the possible diseases that one could get when they had poorly processed chicken. The next step was to ensure that the chickens were raised in a clean environment.

The standards that were set back then are maintained even today by most manufacturers. This ensures that the quality of the meat is high and also that the industry is fine-tuned regularly as per the demands. The people who regulated the industry were always alert to look for unsafe conditions that some farms might be indulging in.

With the increased demands for chicken meat, it became mandatory for the manufacturers to speed up the process of growing the chickens. So, they began to choose breeds that were easier to grow and also breeds that grew faster than the others. The goal was to make as much poultry available as possible in the shortest span of time.

2. The king of meats

It was in the 1980s that chicken meat was declared as the new king of meats. This is when the fast food restaurants also began to demand for chicken meat. The most popular items on the menu included chicken nuggets and also other items that contained tenders of chicken.

The biggest breakthrough in the fast food industry was the introduction of Chicken McNuggets by McDonalds. Towards the end of the year that it was introduced, these nuggets made McDonalds the second largest retailer of chicken meat in the world, next only to KFC. With this sensational item on the menu, even the poultry industry got a tremendous boost.

In less than ten years, the sales of these nuggets increased by 200%. This food item became more than a fad. It was now the staple food for many people in America. In fact it became a way of life for almost all age groups.

In the year 1992, chicken sales reached its peak. For the first time, chicken meat sales were more than beef meat sales. In the year 2001, the revenue from the export of chicken meat reached an all-time high of $2 billion.

Broiler chicken was becoming popular not only in America but also across the globe. With this increase in consumption came another important milestone. The rules became stricter than they had been in the past 6 decades. This was done to ensure the safety of the chickens that were produced mainly for consumption.

The rules played another significant role. By then, several factories that produced chicken meat had been deemed as very unhygienic and inhumane. To ensure that the practises were improved, stricter laws became mandatory.

For the meat that was produced and exported in the US, the rules were laid down by the US Department of Agriculture.

With the introduction of these laws, the cost of the birds also decreased. The number of birds available also increased tremendously. The birds were given a special kind of feed to make their meat better. They were also maintained under very humane conditions and in safer environments.

There are several debates regarding the industry of chicken meat production even today. There is no real law that can define a "humane" environment for these birds. However, all the regulations aim at creating the best conditions for the birds, the workers and the consumers.

3. Chickens as pets

If you are really fond of bird and pets, you would have found the previous section a little under your taste. However, it was a significant part of the history of the domestication of chickens.

Now, the next phase was when people began to view these chickens as worthy companions. Many people raised chickens in their backyards just to keep them company. They were increasingly recognised as pets that could be very entertaining, highly affectionate and of course, a pleasure to have around the family. The responsibilities of having a pet chicken are high. They start from taking care of the little chicks, to housing them and end with keeping them protected from the several predators that are lurking around.

This book is dedicated to all of you who would love to have chickens as pets in your home. The following chapters will take you one step at a time and help you understand what it takes to be the ideal chicken owner.

Chapter 5: Why Choose Chickens as Pets?

The idea of having chickens as pets might seem quite unique. When you look for a domestic pet, you would probably choose furrier options like cats or dogs. However, unknown to most people, chickens can provide a great source of entertainment and companionship. It may seem unreal, however if you ask anyone who owns a pet chicken, you will be surprised at how attached these birds can actually get.

There are several reasons why chickens make great pets. Here are some of the reasons why people actually choose chickens over other pets:

1. They make wonderful pets

They are not the first choice for most people. However, chickens are extremely interactive pets when you keep them with you. If you have raised chickens in your home from the time that they have been chicks, they can be trained and made highly responsive. They will be able to respond to your voice and your moods too. The best thing about having chickens as pets is hand feeding them. It is an absolute joy!

Some breeds of chickens are especially reared to make wonderful pets. Breeds like the Buff Orpington Chicken and the Cochin are very docile and can be really friendly. They are programmed to allow human interaction.

On the other hand, there are other breeds like the Ancona that are a little more anxious and skittish. While these breeds take some time to get used to human companionship, they can be really great when they get used to the people they are around.

It is possible to develop a relationship with your chickens. They can be trained just like any other pets. You need to just give them treats and use consistent commands to make them accustomed to your voice. Then, you will see that they will even flock around you when you call out to them. All you need to do is find a treat that your chicken loves. Their most favourite treat among these birds is white millet. This is nutritious as well as very tasty. When you use treats to communicate with your birds, you will be able to create a bond that is long lasting.

When you are giving them treats, all you need to do is make sure you follow a good diet. You see, chickens will feed on almost anything that you give them. You can even give them chicken scraps that do not contain too much salt. We will discuss the ideal diet for chickens in the following chapters.

Chickens have the ability to follow people around and they will watch your movements. You can pet your chickens, too. They like the occasional pat on the head. But, you must make sure that your bird is not aggressive. You must also never mess with a bird you are unfamiliar with.

Chickens love it when their owners hold them. They feel less stressed and very calm. This is an art that you need to really master or you will leave your chicken feeling aggravated and scared. When you are around your chickens, if you are calm and gentle, they will respond in the same way.

Chickens can also be trained. They will be able to follow commands such as coming to you when you call out. Training is an important part of raising chickens, as they need to have certain behaviour patterns that will suit the environment that they are in. When you start with a chick it is easier to get them used to people and make them more socialized. On the other hand, working with an older chicken is harder. Training a chicken requires a safe environment and a lot of treats.

2. Nutritious eggs

The eggs were the reason why chickens were domesticated in the first place. We all know of the nutritional value of chicken eggs.

Buff Orpington Chickens are prolific egg layers, laying about 200 eggs each year.

Imagine if you have a small flock, you will have enough eggs to take care of your family's needs completely. For instance, having about 5 Buff Orpington Chickens means that you can easily get 200 to 250 eggs each year.

Of course, the quality of the eggs that you get in your backyard is much better than the ones that you buy at stores. The nutritional value of these eggs is greater as they are fresh. Additionally, the eggs that are available commercially are highly processed. The nutritional value and quality of these eggs are most often tampered with.

In some facilities, the eggs are produced by molting the flocks. Sometimes the eggs are even kept in coolers and refrigerators before they are processed. In any case, the processed eggs have much lesser nutritional value in comparison to the ones that you will get in your home.

The soil that is present on the eggs is removed using detergents. These eggs are then inspected visually and packed according to their quality. There are certain standards that are used to categorize these eggs. These standards have been set by the USDA. If you notice the packaging of the eggs, you will see three grades: A, AA and B. these grades are set after inspecting the egg thoroughly. The factors are decided as follows:

- AA Quality:
- Shell clean
- No breakage on shell
- Air cell less than $1/8^{th}$ inch in depth
- Clear and firm egg white
- Perfect yolk.

- A Quality
- Clean Shell
- No Breakage

- Air cell not more than 3/16th inch in depth
- Air cell should be free
- White clear and reasonably firm
- Yolk outline defined well

- B Quality:
- Egg should be unbroken
- Slight abnormality permitted
- May have stains on surface
- Stains cannot cover more than 1/32 of the surface when concentrated.
- Stains cannot cover more than 1/16th of the surface if scattered
- Prominent dirt and stains not allowed
- Air cell should be around 3/16th in depth.
- White slightly watery and weak
- Yolk appears dark and enlarged or flattened.
- The yolk may have slight defects as long as it's edible.

However, the eggs that you can get in your home are no match to these store bought eggs.

3. To breed

Breeding chickens is a very popular and a rather important business today. Individuals who rear chickens to breed keep them for two purposes. The first one is to create more specimens of the same bloodline. Then, they can also create a new breed that retains certain qualities that you consider desirable. This includes details like egg of a particular size, the bird of a particular color or even a certain behaviour pattern that you consider desirable in chickens.

If you are interested in keeping chickens to breed them, then you can get a lot of information from local breeders who have been doing this for a profession. If you are interested in a particular breed, you will be able to find poultry farms or breeders who specialise in that breed as well.

There are several books and websites that can give you ample information as well. These websites contain details about selling and showing the breeds. They will also be able to help you with all the information that you need on the supplies and the products available on the market.

Most individuals who keep chickens at home for breeding purposes prefer creating hybrids. This involves cross breeding purebred chickens. This requires a couple of trials till you have all the traits that you are looking for in that bird.

When you see that your flock size is increasing too fast and you do not want to keep all the birds, you always have the option of selling them or simply giving them away to people. You may also donate chickens to farms nearby. There are special websites that are dedicated to poultry sales. You also have the option of putting up advertisements on these websites.

Most of these websites are free. These websites also allow you to sell related products and services. You may also look for services that you require. All you need to do is type in your ZIP code and you will find vendors near your home.

If you are an amateur, you need not worry. There are several breeds that you can mix to create beautiful off springs. The only thing that you need to keep in mind is that you must never mix breeds that have even the slightest problem. If you notice even small issues like the abundance of the feathers, the shape of the beak etc. you must reconsider using a certain specimen.

There are several options available with respect to the kinds of breeds that are most compatible. All you need to do is read up a little bit about these breeds and then you are good to start experimenting.

4. To Sell

Chickens are a very good option if you are looking at selling them. You see, there are several farms and also individuals who are looking at buying a beautiful chicken to take home. If you are thinking of breeding chickens then selling is much easier as you will always have a flock that is increasing in number.

Before you look at selling your chickens, you must check with your local authorities about the laws involving chicken sales. You can check with the department of agriculture or even the City Hall for more details about selling your chickens. If there are any laws preventing the sale of certain breeds, you must be aware. Once you have this clear, you need to look for avenues to sell your chickens. While the most effective one is word of mouth, you can also look at putting up posts on ecommerce websites. Even your local classifieds should allow you to place advertisements about selling your birds.

When you are selling your chickens, make sure that you only pick the ones that are healthy. This will ensure that you maintain a good reputation in the market. Make sure you provide the following details when you are selling your bird:

- The Age of the bird
- The breed
- They egg production capacity
- The frequency of health
- Health problems if any

On an average, a healthy chicken should fetch you anything between $1 and $5. The cost of the bird depends entirely on the gender and the breed. Of course, the females are more expensive than the males. If you have a rare breed, you can sell it for a higher price too. For instance, breeds like Pullets can cost anything between $15 and $25.

If you are selling your chicken for the first time, you may not know how to price the bird. You can actually do a small survey to see what price other breeders are selling them at. Chickens that are old and unproductive should be sold for a lesser cost always. You must try to sell these off your farm as soon as you can. Any bird that is sick or weak should not be sold. This is because the bird looks unfit at the first glance if it really does have any disorder.

5. For Showing

There are several individuals who simply love to showcase their birds. Whether they are breeders or just pet owners, showing the birds at state fairs and in special poultry exhibitions is a matter of great pride. For those who are interested in showing the birds, the care that they need to take is a little more. The bird needs to be maintained as per the standards recommended by the American Poultry Association.

While exhibitions give you a great opportunity to actually groom and take care of your chicken, the other advantage is that you also get to learn a lot from shows. You will have the opportunity of meeting several individuals who are interested in breeding and raising chickens. They will be able to share several tips and ideas that will help you provide a better environment for your chickens to thrive in. If you are selling, shows are a great place to showcase your specimens. If they are good quality show birds, they can fetch you a handsome price.

Irrespective of the reason for rearing the chicken, the most important thing is that you must be willing to take the responsibility of these birds. Once you do that, you will be able to experience a completely different kind of bond. These birds are entirely different from the regular domestic pets. And, that is what makes them so special.

Chapter 6: Bringing Home Buff Orpington Chickens

The most important thing that you need to do when you decide to bring home a pet chicken is figure out where to get it from in the first place. However, even more important than that, know what kind of chicken you want to bring home. At what stage of life should that chicken be introduced into your home?

Before you get into the details of getting a chicken home, I would like to familiarize you with some common terminologies associated with chickens. This will help you understand what exactly a breeder or a seller is trying to set you up with.

- **Chick:** This is a baby chicken
- **Hen:** This is a fully grown, female chicken
- **Rooster:** This is a fully grown, male chicken
- **Pullet:** This is a female that is less than one year of age
- **Cockerel:** This is a male that is less than one year of age
- **Capon:** A male chicken that has been castrated

When you go shopping for a feathered companion, you can be quite overwhelmed. You can be sure of the breed that you want to buy when you are sure of why you are getting that bird in the first place. As we discussed before, there are several reasons why you may want a chicken. Depending on that you can choose not only the breed but also the age of the bird that you bring home. Even with the age, you have three options:

1. Bring home eggs

The earlier you start, the better it is. If you want to be really bonded with your pet chicken, you can choose to raise it from the time when it is an egg. Starting at this stage has several rewards.

If you have children at home, this is a particularly interesting option.

You need to bring home a fertilized egg and it will develop each day in the shell. The entire process should take about 21 days. If you already have a hen and a rooster, then you will able to hatch the egg naturally. On the other hand when you have only an egg, you need to use a process called candling to hatch your egg.

We will discuss this process in detail. However, as of now let us look at this process in brief. You need to place the egg in a heated environment that is similar to the mother's. For this you have several types of incubators that you can use. You need to make sure that you turn the egg every day to make sure that the embryo forms properly. You can choose mechanical incubators if you feel like it is too much work

However, this is a process that requires a great deal of patience. Not every egg that you bring home will hatch as expected. You see, the embryo is extremely delicate. There are several reasons why the egg may not hatch.

When you have kids at home, you need to be particularly careful as there may be several disappointments with the cracked eggs. You must never tell them how many eggs you brought to prevent any sadness. You can even ask the kids to follow the growth of the chicks inside the egg and predict if they will hatch or not. This activity prepares the kids for a possibility that all the eggs will not hatch. You must always focus on the positivity of the process. Of course, you want to see the eggs hatch and hear the chirping of little birds. However, you must understand that this is a lot of work. If you can be prepared for that, you can enjoy a lifetime of love and companionship.

2. Baby Chicks

This is the second option that you will have in front of you. This is the best option available if you do not have the time to actually hatch the eggs. You can buy a chick that is one day old or even opt for one that is a couple of days old.

There are several places where you can get your chicks from. Most pet owners these days prefer to get their chicks online. There are several reliable online hatcheries where you can get the birds of your choice.

When you are looking at buying chicks online, you need to do a good amount of research. Some of these online stores will have certain terms and conditions. The most common condition is that you need to buy a minimum number. This number starts at 25 usually. If you make the commitment and are unable to care for so many chickens, you will end up in trouble.

The chicks are only shipped after they are at least a day old. This is when they have had enough food to keep themselves warm during the journey. These chicks are shipped to your home using services like the US postal service. They require special handling as well.

You can expect your pets to reach you in about three days' time. This information is given to you prior so that you can collect your chickens. If you are not available to collect the chickens, they will be left waiting in the post office without food or water.

When you are ordering off the Internet, you also need to consider the weather conditions. If it is too hot or too cold, you will not be able to get them shipped from most hatcheries. Make sure you order them only when you have enough time on your hands to collect them on time.

When you go to collect your package, make sure you open and check if the chicks are alive. This is a policy that you need to pay great attention to. Most hatcheries will have all the terms and conditions regarding such an untoward incident mentioned on their website. You can also issue a claim at the post office if you feel like your chicks have not been handled correctly.

With purchases that are made online, one needs to be extremely careful about where he is ordering from. Make sure you check all the reviews and testimonials correctly before you actually place the order. You can also get recommendations from friends and other chicken owners.

If you are certain that a certain website is completely reliable, you may go for it. If not, you must be open to other options to obtain your chickens. You can be sure that a website is reliable if they have contact numbers that you can dial to speak with them. If they sound professional and are willing to answer all your queries and issues, you can rest assured. On the other hand, if they seem hesitant in providing you with the details that you are looking for, you must think twice before making an investment.

The other option is to go in person and pick up the chicks. There are several local farms and cooperatives where chicks are sold. You can even buy them from your local pet store. In most of these commercial areas, you will be able to find baby chicks around Easter. In fact, springtime is the best season to bring home chickens.

When you go in person, you can be a lot more confident of the quality of the chickens that you are bringing home. If you notice any dead chicks in the place where you plan to buy the chickens from, just turn around and walk home. If the chicken's cages have too much fecal build up, it is an indication that the chicks may be carrying deadly diseases. Even then, you must look for another option.

There are several preparations that you need to make before you bring the chicks home. If they are being shipped to your home, you must understand that they have gone through a lot of stress. So, they will need a warm resting spot when they are back. This spot should be a proper warmer in which you can control the temperature. The temperature must be maintained at about 90 degrees and the light should always be kept on.

You must have plenty of water available for the chicks to drink. Of course, you cannot place your water in deep bowls as the chicks are too small. They even run the risk of drowning in the bowl if it is too deep. You need to use small and shallow cups that they can drink from comfortably. The water must be changed on a regular basis to make sure that there is no infection or contamination.

Most often, the chicks are so little that they do not even know how to drink water. If you notice that one of your chicks is not drinking the water that you have placed, you must lead it to the bowl so it can start drinking.

The next thing that you need to worry about is the feed. There may not be commercially prepared starter food at your home. Do not worry. All you need is some infant cereal or even instant oatmeal. After this you can get special mash that is meant for baby chicks.

You must remember that chicks are extremely delicate. So, you must not handle them too much. Even if you need to pick them up and check on them, you need to be extremely cautious. There are several reasons why you need to handle the chicks. You may have to change the location or even clean the vent.

Baby chicks are extremely cute and you may want to fondle them and really cuddle. However, remember that you must handle them only when it is absolutely necessary. Otherwise, you must leave them alone. Your baby chick will be stronger in a couple of days. That is when you can take them out and play with them.

3. Cockerels and Pullets

If you are a first time owner, pullets and cockerels are the best option for you. They are less than one year old. This is the age when they are not as tender and delicate as the baby chicks. On the other hand, they are not grown up enough to be on their own.

At that age, they do not need constant attention like the baby chicks. Since they have ample feathers to keep themselves warm, you need not worry about them catching some deadly disease or falling sick. They are also structurally stronger which means that you need not worry about handling them too much or causing them any damage.

The good news with pullets and cockerels is that they must have already started laying eggs. Usually, chickens are able to lay eggs when they are about 4 months old. So, if you are interested in a lucrative egg business, this is the best age for you.

The age of the chicken is a very important factor in deciding how the environment in your home will be. If you are purchasing a baby chick, the preparations are a lot more. On the other hand an adult will only require a good enough coop. The next set of questions that you need to ask yourself is the more practical one. When you are buying chickens, only the age is not a deciding factor. There are several other things that determine where you will buy the chicks from and how you plan to take care of them. Here are some more things that you could consider when you are out there shopping for your feathered friends.

4. Where to get good Buff Orpington Chickens

When you have decided to bring home Buff Orpington Chickens, the next question is where to get them from? There are several options that are available to anyone who is interested in purchasing chickens. Here are some places where you will definitely be able to get healthy Buff Orpington Chickens:

Online

To begin with, there are many websites where you will regularly find Buff Orpington Chickens on sale. These websites may belong to popular pet stores or even hatcheries. Sometimes, they might even be exclusive online stores that are meant to sell chickens. There are several advantages of choosing your pet online. You do not have to make painful trips to hatcheries that are located really far away from the city most of the time. Additionally, you will also be able to find great discounts when you buy your chickens online.

Of course, the disadvantages are also present. You will have to rely on the seller's word as you will not be able to go and physically examine the birds when you make a purchase. This can be quite misleading. In addition to that, the shipping is always a risk to the health of little baby birds. Most often, they die if the travel distance is too long.

So, if you are really considering buying a chicken online, make sure that you either shop from the websites of popular stores or that you look for recommendations from people who have made online purchases before. Unless you are completely sure of the authenticity and the reliability of a website, do not make any payments even if you feel like the costs are more than reasonable.

Hatcheries

A hatchery is a special facility where eggs are incubated and hatched artificially. This is a really booming industry especially for poultry and fish. The idea with hatcheries is to breed varieties that are rare or unusual for a specific region.

With special breeds like the Buff Orpington Chickens, you will be able to find several hatcheries that focus on this breed. There are two types of hatcheries. There is one that produces eggs at the hatchery through natural insemination and the other one that produces eggs through artificial insemination. The latter usually focuses on the hybrids.

When you visit a hatchery to buy your chickens, make sure that you check the quality of the eggs thoroughly before your make a purchase. You must be sure that the eggs are cleaned well before they are put into the incubator. They must also be checked well for soundness before they are incubated. The conditions of incubation must also be healthy. That is when you can be assured that the chickens that you take home will remain healthy.

Ask for a health certificate for the poultry that is sold to you. In most hatcheries, the chicks are vaccinated within a few days of hatching. You must also check for this before you buy the chicks so that you know if you will have to take them to the vet before you take them home.

Poultry Organisations

There are several national and local poultry organisations where you can pick up your chickens. These organisations usually focus on producing birds that are of show quality.

There are also several Buff Orpington Chicken Clubs and Associations that you will be able to locate in your zip code. The advantage of buying in these clubs is that you will have beautiful chickens that are maintained as per all the standards recommended by the American Poultry Association.

Of course, the birds that you buy from such places might seem really expensive. However, for those of you who have business interests in keeping the poultry, it is an investment that is completely worth it. You can check on the APA website for details on the recommended standards so that you do not end up paying too much for a bird that is nowhere near show standards.

Breeders

With popular breeds like the Buff Orpington Chickens, there will be several individual breeders who will be able to get you healthy specimens for your home. The advantages of getting a chicken from a good breeder are many, especially if you are a first time chicken owner.

When you have a reliable breeder to help you out, he will become the best consultant next to your veterinarian with respect to proper care for your birds. Breeders will also be able to help you convert your hobby into a lucrative business, as they will be able to provide you with leads for your sales.

When you buy from an individual breeder, make sure that you visit his set up once before you buy your beloved pet. The most important thing is the condition in which your breeder is hatching and raising the chicks. If you see that the coops have not been cleaned for a long time, you must be very careful. Especially, feces deposited around the nests means that the chicks could be harboring dangerous diseases. If you already have a flock of your own, you will be jeopardising the health of the entire flock if you neglect this important part.

Your breeder must also be able to provide you with a health certificate for the chicks that you buy. If the breeder is hesitant to provide you with one, it is recommended that you look for another one who is okay with giving you a certificate.

Whenever you go to a local breeder, look for recommendations. If you are new to rearing chickens, speak to friends or relatives who have already had chickens at home. They should be able to help you out. You may even want to take someone reliable with you when you go to a breeder for the first time. That way even the breeder will be aware that you know what you are talking about and that he cannot get away with giving you unhealthy birds for your home.

Rescue Shelters

Another interesting option is adopting birds for your backyard. This is considered an extremely humane option as there are several birds who really require care and help. The best part about this is also that you can bring home the chickens for free!

If you have decided to adopt chicks or even an adult hen or rooster, here are a few steps that you need to take in order to actually bring home the bird of your choice.

The first thing that you need to do is contact your local authorities about adoption in your state. There are some rules that you will need to abide by depending upon the part of the world that you are residing in. In some zones, adoption is not as easy as picking a bird and bringing it home. You need to get a few permits and licenses for your backyard poultry. If you are looking at a business with the chickens that you are adopting, there may be several more rules that are applicable to you.

The next thing is to look for an organisation that is putting chickens or adult birds up for adoption. You can ask for assistance at veterinary hospitals or even your local municipality. There are several rescue shelters in each area. If you are still unable to find a good place, just look online. The other advice I have is for you to look in the agricultural or rural areas. You are most likely to find great options in these areas.

When you have chosen an organisation that you want to adopt from, you can send in a request. The best thing to do would be to actually visit the place to adopt your chickens. You must be prepared for a full-fledged interview when you are out to adopt a Buff Orpington Chicken. The thing is most of these shelters want to ensure that the birds that they recue do not go back to living in cruel conditions. They will, therefore, ask you about the space that you have to accommodate the birds, details about your other pets, your source of funds to support the chickens that you are adopting etc. So, if you are going to adopt a bird, there are things that you want to consider before you meet the authorities.

If you show the slightest signs of hesitation or lack of knowledge, your chances of bringing home those beautiful birds are greatly reduced. Now, you definitely do not want that to happen, do you?

Once you have convincingly answered all the questions, you will be allowed to take a look at the birds that are up for adoption. When you have found the ones that you think you want to take home, you can fix a date and time when you want to pick up the birds. When you have finalised on the birds, make sure you ask about the fees, if any. Sometimes, there is a small municipality fee that you will have to pay before you adopt a bird. However, in most cases, adoption is free.

It is a good thing to adopt multiple chicks at one time. That way, you will be able to give your feathered companions some friends to hang around with while you are out or away at work.

No matter what option you choose with respect to bringing home a chicken, you must be fully aware that the responsibility that you will have is very high. You must be prepared to transform parts of your home into suitable environments for these beautiful birds that you will be sharing your home with.

If you already have poultry or other pets at home, the challenges that you will face are different. While you would have decent experience with respect to the care that the birds need, you will have to worry about things like ensuring that the animals and birds in your home are able to live together comfortably.

For first time owners, everything from just buying the bird is a challenge that you have to overcome. While this journey is actually a lot of fun, it can be overwhelming if you do not have the right assistance.

This book is designed to help you overcome these challenges. Of course, the first thing that you will need help with is understanding how much you can handle. There are several considerations before you actually welcome a pet chicken into your home.

There are some very important questions that you need to ask yourself before you go out there to buy or adopt chickens. The next part of this chapter will help you find the answers to these questions as well. Only when you are convinced about your choice of having chickens as pets should you take up this big responsibility.

5. Considerations before bringing home a chicken

Do you really find them appealing?

If you are planning to bring home a chicken, just because your friends or members of your family think that they make great pets, reconsider your choice. Before you bring home a chicken, you must make sure that you have enough experience with actually being around them.

Try to spend some time with pets that your friends may have. If not, you could also spend some time at local farms and agricultural areas to get a little more insight into what it actually takes to have chickens at home. If you feel like they do not particularly appeal to you, reconsider your choice.

If you feel less inclined towards petting or taking care of your chicken, it is not a good thing for either you or the chicken. Also, if you have a partner, spouse or family member who does not exactly love chickens, you must still reconsider your choice. Remember, any negativity towards a pet can be really stressful for them.

Will you have enough time?

Most people think that having pets like chickens is not as time consuming. After all, they do not need to be walked every day. They will also hang around with their flock and find ways to keep themselves entertained. If you think the same, then, a chicken is not the best pet for your home!

Although it may seem easy to keep flocks at home, the truth is that they require a lot of care of a daily basis. Of course, this care does include feeding and making sure that they have enough water to drink. However, there is more that you need to worry about. You will have to collect the eggs often. You will have to clean the coop of your beloved pet. In case you have a broody hen, the care that is required is quite different.

So, when you think about it, you at least need to spend a couple of hours every day with your chickens to ensure that they are happy and healthy. If you have a job that demands a lot of time, you must not consider having pets at all. If you travel frequently, you will have to think of ways to ensure that the chickens get the care that they need on a daily basis.

As you go through this book, you will understand why I insist on having enough time for the birds that you plan to bring home. If you cannot make time for them, you will definitely jeopardize the health and well-being of the birds.

How much space do you have?

Most people think of chickens as the perfect backyard, urban pets as they really don't require as much space as other pets. Usually, they will stick to their coop or the other forms of housing that you may provide them with. Remember that even the coop needs to be spacious enough. On an average, every chicken should have at least 10 feet of space for itself.

On the other hand, if you plan to have free range chickens that can roam around freely, the coop requirements are lesser. However, it means that you need to have a big enough yard for the birds to move around in. If you are in an apartment, you will really have to worry about space issues.

Chickens are always healthier if they have enough space to move around outdoors. They love to forage and walk around in the open at every chance that they get. This is their natural way of getting the exercise that they need. They will also be less stressed and anxious if they have enough outdoor space to move around in.

The other factor that you must consider is that the more space they have outdoors, the safer your property indoors is. Chickens love to scratch the ground or forage for insects. If they are not left outdoors to fulfil this behavioural need, then you will have to come to terms with the fact that they will replace fresh outdoor soil with your carpet or sofa.

So, if you are bringing home a pet chicken, make sure that you will be able to provide it with an ambience that it can grow healthily in. There is no point in depriving a chicken of its basic survival needs and stripping it of its natural instincts. That is not only harmful for the bird but may also lead to unwanted property destruction!

Are you allowed to have chickens?

There are several licenses that are required to keep poultry in your backyard. We will discuss these licenses in detail in the following chapter. However, before that you need to check if your local area authorities even allow you to have poultry in the backyard.

If you are living in an apartment, you will have to check with the concerned board about the regulations about keeping chickens or any pets, in general. If they have any objection to it, it is best that you avoid any unwanted issues.

There are ways to keep chickens as pets legally. For this you will have to go through all the guidelines pertaining to keeping chickens as pets in your home as well as in the area that you live in.

Ask thy neighbors.

Whenever you bring home pets, always check with your neighbors to ensure that you are not causing any form of inconvenience to them. Chickens are not particularly noisy. However, if one of your chicks turns out to be a rooster, you are in for some trouble.

You may also have neighbors who are allergic to chickens. IF you think that there are any chances of your chickens wandering off into the neighbors yard, inform them. Of course, you must take precautions to ensure that this does not happen. Another problem that may arise with chickens that wander away is the eggs. Your neighbors will most certainly not be pleased about having broken eggs in their yard. So as general courtesy, make sure that you check with your neighbors.

Consider the costs

The only thing that you will get for free when you keep chickens at home is the eggs. Besides that, everything else will come with a price attached to it. I will give you a detailed breakdown of the costs towards the end of this book. However, I would like to prepare you in advance for the high maintenance costs involved with pets. If you feel like you have trouble with making ends meet, you must never opt for keeping chickens at home. They can really take up a big chunk of your funds.

Your geographic location

The place that you live in is important to decide which chicken breed that you will bring into your home. There are various chicken breeds that are unable to thrive in extreme cold and hot weather conditions. On the other hand, there are some breeds that are cold or heat hardy. Depending upon your geographic location, you can decide which breed you want to bring home.

In case you live in a place that gets really cold, you must consider bringing home standard breeds instead of the Buff Orpington Chickens. When you are out purchasing your chickens, study the combs and the wattles. The smaller they are, the better it is for a cold condition. When the combs or Buff Orpington Chickens are smaller, it means that the particular breed is less susceptible to frost bites.

On the other hand, if the place that you live in has very hot weather conditions, there are other features that you must look for. Never buy the fluffy breeds. If they have feathered feet, they will find it especially hard to thrive in very hot conditions. As a thumb rule, the Buff Orpington Chickens survive the heat better.

You see, the Buff Orpington Chickens usually have large combs and really close feathering that will keep them insulated against the heat. There are special European breeds known as the naked necks that are really great for the hot climates. These birds have fewer feathers and are therefore more accustomed to the hot climates.

In case you are very fond of a particular breed that may not be suitable for the weather conditions of your place, you can create an artificial environment. This means that you can have temperature controlled coops and housing that these birds can live in comfortably.

Creating an artificial environment is quite expensive. Additionally, it also means that the birds will not grow to be at the peak of health. So, it is always better to choose breeds that are naturally adaptable to the climatic conditions of the place that you are living in.

Why do you want chickens?

This is perhaps the most important question that you will be asking yourself before bringing home chickens. If you can find the answer to this question, you will be able to decide which breed suits you the best.

If you are simply looking at having companions or pets, you should choose the gentler and calmer breeds. They will also be more personable which means that you can train them to obey commands or even perform some simple tricks.

For those who are looking at a lucrative egg business, breeds like the Buff Orpington Chicken are ideal. These birds are prolific egg layers and will be able to help you make a really big profit if they are raised in healthy conditions.

Lastly, if you are looking at buying chickens for meat production, you must choose breeds that grow faster. Those breeds will be better as the quality and quantity of the meat that you get will be really good.

Should you get a rooster?

If you are a first time chicken owner, then a rooster may not be the best choice for you. They can be really noisy as pets which can be quite a problem with neighbors. If you think that roosters only crow at the break of dawn, then you are highly mistaken. They crow all day long.

Of course they are gorgeous. If that is the only reason you want to have them, then think about it again. You see, with the process of artificial insemination available as an option, it is no longer necessary to have a rooster. When you have ample experience with hens and chickens, you can think about bringing home a rooster.

Once you have answered all these questions, you are ready to make a commitment to a chicken. You will be better prepared to take care of all the needs of your pet chicken and you will also be able to provide them with the best living conditions.

Chapter 7: Preparing Your Home For Chickens

A chicken is quite different from a regular pet that you would bring home. For instance, it is more common for people to have a dog or a cat in their home. However, a chicken might seem unusual. If you are not completely prepared for it, you may experience a lot of issues when you bring home a pet chicken. So there are some things that you need to do in advance before you make your home a safe haven for chickens.

1. Preparing the family

Your entire family needs to be aware of the responsibility that comes with having pet Buff Orpington Chickens at home. Since these pets are not your ordinary fuzzy and furry pets, you need to understand that your family also needs some getting used to. If you simply love the idea of having a chicken at home, here are some tips that will help you make your family enjoy the whole process as well:

• First talk to your family about your pet choice. If you have an enthusiastic family, this may not be much trouble. However, if you feel like your family is sceptical about the whole idea, you may want to give them some information on why having a pet chicken can actually be advantageous.

• Check your family for allergies. You must be sure that your family does not have any member who is allergic to chickens. If you have been frequently visiting farms and agricultural areas, you might already be familiar with the allergies present in your family. On the other hand, if you think that not everyone has had as much experience with poultry as yourself, you might want them to get tested by experts.

• If you have a family member who does not approve of this idea, reconsider the option of bringing home a chicken.

• If you are certain that you will be bringing home a pet chicken, choose the breed that you want to bring home along with your entire family. It is quite fun to go out to various hatcheries and farms to check out the breeds that are available. This is especially important if you have kids in your home. They must be part of the entire decision making process so that they feel a sense of responsibility towards the pet.

• Involve your family in the knowledge gaining process. Watch informative videos, make small notes or even read books together. The more everyone knows about poultry care, the better it is for you and your new pet. Gather as much information as you can about the proper caring methods for chickens.

• Make sure that they are all present when you bring home the chickens for the first time. This will make them involved in the process of raising the chickens right from the beginning.

• Assign responsibilities to each member of the family. Again, this is particularly important if you have children at home. They need to understand the fact that having chickens at home is not just fun and games. Give them simple tasks like feeding the birds. Kids must never be given the job of cleaning as they may catch serious infections and diseases.

• Make sure that everyone in your family is aware of how to handle the chickens properly. Especially if you are bringing home small baby chicks, they need to be taken care of rather delicately. If your family keeps on touching them and fondling them, they will get anxious and, in worst cases, injured.

• If there are children at home, tell them that the new pet is not a toy. Your child must never tease or trouble the bird. While something as simple as a pat on the head is permissible, make sure that kids do not kiss or hug the birds too close. There are serious infections that may be transmitted to children. Also, if the bird is slightly older, it may harm the child in the process of defending itself. Never let the child pull the feathers or even squeeze the birds too hard. While they may seem cute and cuddly, hens and roosters can be nasty when they are defensive.

2. The initial days

The first few days can be really hard for your Buff Orpington Chickens and you. When they have just arrived in your home, it is natural for you to feel all excited and a little nervous, of course. You may spend the first few days obsessing about the behavior of your flock and you can never be certain if they are behaving in the right way or not because you are not sure if you have provided them with the perfect ambience to thrive well in. So in the first few days, here are some tips that will really help you:

• Leave them alone for a while. If you are keeping them indoors, especially, the last thing that you want to worry about is predators. Allow your Buff Orpington Chickens to explore the area that they are going to live in for the next few years of their lives. If you are constantly checking on them, they may not be able to do this comfortably.

• The next thing that you need to do is make sure that they have a warm and comfortable space to be in. You may also have to place a small lamp in their coop to provide them with ample warmth if they are still baby chicks. We will get into the details in the next part of this chapter.

• Chickens can be overwhelmed easily. So if you have a pet at home, keep it away from your chicken for the first few days. Also avoid loud noises and sounds around the new members of your family. You definitely do not want to have them associating you with dreadful noises.

- If they are not eating properly or are very quiet, leave them alone. They are probably tired from the journey if they have been shipped. In case you have shifted them to a new coop or room as well, they will be too scared to even eat properly.

- Sometimes they may begin to lay eggs and suddenly stop. This is perfectly normal.

- The eggs may also have very soft shells. This is not a medical issue if it does not continue for too long. If the size and quality of the egg resorts to normal, it means that your chicken is just stressed about the new environment that it has suddenly been brought into.

- Keep an eye on your chickens. Always observe their behaviour.

3. Introducing your chickens to an existing flock

The hardest part about bringing home chickens is introducing them to a flock that is already in your home. The reason this is so hard is that when you try to mix different breeds of hens in one flock, there are chances of fights and squabbles. You need to be extremely careful to ensure the safety of the new birds and also the safety of the birds in your current flock. If you have two males, especially, the issues are a lot more than you can imagine.

In the wild, chickens usually live in smaller groups. So, it is best that you maintain this even when you have chickens in your backyard. When you are introducing new chickens to your flock, there are several things that could go wrong unless you get the introduction right.

In order to get the introduction right, you need to understand a natural process known as "the pecking order". In fact, the pecking order is so important in hens that the word "hen pecked" actually originated from here.

Flock Dynamics

Chickens look like really pleasant creatures. So, it is natural for most owners to think that when you bring home a chicken and introduce it to the existing flock, they will simply get along with each other and miraculously become one happy family.

Well, most chicken owners wish that the process was that simple. Especially with breeds like the Buff Orpington Chickens, this is a matter of great concern. So before you just give your existing flock new "friends", you may want to take a couple of important precautions.

When there is a flock that already exists in your home, you need to understand that there are some flock dynamics that have already been established. Each hen or rooster in that group has its own personality. Hence, the order in which they dominate the group has already been established. There is always one bird that is the leader or the most dominant one in the group. This order of dominance is maintained and the bird that is the least dominant is placed in the end.

Most often, the rooster is the most dominant one in the group and the least dominant one is the meekest one in the group. In an established group, the older chickens will always be a lot more dominant.

Chickens have a certain way of deciding the order that they will dominate in. Of course, there is no prize for guessing how they pick this order. As the name suggests, the chickens will decide who is the strongest of them all by, well, pecking. You will also notice the following behaviour patterns among birds when they try to establish the pecking order:

- They will squabble
- They will block access to food and water
- They will chase the weaker birds
- They will fight
- They will bump chests
- They will also "thrash talk" in a way.

The basic idea is that they need to make life miserable for the birds that they consider as lower or weaker. When the weaker bird caves in, the pecking order gets established. Sometimes, the pecking order is established in just a few days. In other cases, it may take close to two weeks to properly establish this order.

In case the Buff Orpington Chickens that you introduce to your flock are also extremely dominating, you are asking for some trouble. They will begin to compete with one another almost instantly to get their position as the most dominating bird. Sometimes, this squabbling can get really ugly leaving the birds injured or even dead!

If you have a flock where the pecking order is being established, you can be assured that it is not the prettiest thing you will see. However, you must allow this process to take place as this is the only way that you can have a peaceful flock in your home.

You see, only when you have a fully established flock in your home will the quarrels be minimum. Every bird will know its place in the flocks and they will, very seldom, try to claim a better spot. All the disputes that arose with the introduction of the new birds will be fully settled.

When the pecking order has been set in a group, it is much easier as the disputes arising in the future will also be quickly solved, thanks to the hierarchy. If, at this point, you are thinking that chickens are ridiculously ambitious creatures, you will be surprised to know that even other animals like wolves have a pecking order in their groups. This is the only way that the group can function as a unit.

So, whenever you plan to add a new chicken to your flock, you can do nothing more than endure the fighting and the squabbling. However, always make it a point to observe your flock well. If you notice serious injuries or very aggressive fights, you may consider taking the new chickens out of the flock for a while. There are many issues that you must consider when you introduce a new chicken to the flock. I have provided a list below. Make sure you give each one serious thought to ensure the best health for your flock.

• Quarantining: Although most new chickens look healthy from the outside, there are chances that they will destroy your entire flock if you are not careful enough. So, when you are introducing a new bird into your flock, make sure that you take all the quarantining measures necessary. The best thing to do would be to keep the new chickens in a separate space for two weeks. Observe them to make sure that they do not ruin the well-being of the existing flock.

• Size matters: If you are adding a Buff Orpington Chicken to a group of large birds, it might be an issue. Similarly, if you add a younger bird, you may see that he will get bullied by the birds. So, when you are adding a new bird to the flock, make sure that he is a fully mature bird that is of a decent size.

• Distract the existing flock: If the birds in your existing flock have something new to catch their attention, they may not trouble the new bird as much. You could add a shiny object or even a few spring greens to spare your newcomers the tension.

• Keep them divided: It is a good idea to use a make shift fence when you are introducing a new bird to the flock. This will give them a safe space in which they can get accustomed to the existing birds. Even the existing flock will become used to the sights and sounds of the newcomers.

• Make sure there is enough food: If the food containers are plenty, there will be fewer reasons to squabble and fight. Also, the new chickens are often scared. So, they need to have enough food that they know that they can eat safely. If you cannot ensure this, they will probably just stick to their part of the coop and never get out.

• Make enough room: If your chickens have enough space, they will not get in each other's face. You can even let the flock out in the open for a while. This will help the birds that are getting pecked run away to a safer spot, thus avoiding serious injuries.

• No Blood: The one personality quirk that chickens have is that they love to peck at the wounds that are still fresh. If you see that there is a bird that has been wounded, you must take him out of the coop immediately. Even a small amount of blood means that the entire flock will actually peck the wounded bird to death!

• Keeping cocks together: We have all heard of cocks fighting quite aggressively. So if you are introducing a cock to a flock that already has cocks in it, you might have to take a lot of precautions. The best thing to do is to place the younger cocks with the older ones in a pen for a while. The older cocks actually teach the youngsters how to behave!

• Introductions at night: if you plan to introduce the new chickens to the flock at night or when it is dark, make sure that you are almost at the break of dawn. If the current flock wakes up to a new member suddenly, they may become so overwhelmed that they will peck the newcomer to death.

• Keep the age groups different: This is a pretty important tip. To begin with, the older chickens tend to be a lot more dominating. Additionally, there may also be some infections within a group that the younger chickens are not immune to.

The best introductions:

If you plan to introduce new hens to the group, the best way to do it would be to actually place the newer chickens in a fenced area in the run that your current flock is already using. This approach is best preferred as the new chickens have a space that they can be safe in. At the same time, they will face the existing birds regularly. When this type of interaction occurs, both the groups feel less threatened in each other's presence. Eventually, they will get accustomed to the sights and sounds of each other and will be less aggressive when they are placed in the same house together.

Another approach that is rather interesting is placing both groups in a new house and a new run. Since the space is new to both the groups, the pecking order has still not been established. The process of establishing the order will not change much. However, the level of aggression will be much lesser when the hens are introduced in a completely new environment. All you need to do is ensure that they have ample space for themselves. You must also provide your chickens with enough food so that they do not have too many reasons to be aggressive.

Sometimes, there might be one particular bird that is extremely aggressive. If you are able to identify this bird, you must take it away from the group. It is alright even if this bird belongs to your existing flock. That way, it will become easier for the pecking order to be established in the group. When you know that your current group of birds are living together in peace, reintroduce the aggressive bird. Now, he is the newcomer and will be toned down by the established pecking order.

Sometimes, it may seem like a lot of effort when you try to introduce a new bunch of chickens to an existing flock. However, you do not have too many options when you are in a chicken business. You must always rotate your flock. While this may seem challenging in the beginning. It will be a walk in the park as you progress and get used to the process.

4. Introducing your chickens to pets

Another matter of great concern is introducing your Buff Orpington Chicken to the pets that you have at home. There are two possibilities when you bring home a chicken. Your existing pets will become great friends with it, or, they will be foes! Either way, you need to introduce your chickens to your family pets.

Think of introducing pets to chickens as introducing a new baby brother or sister to a child. Of course, there will be an initial phase of tantrum throwing and jealousy. However, as time goes on, things will be alright. All you need to do is supervise the toddler and the infant during this period of acclimatization.

If you have a pet that you keep indoors, you may argue that it is not necessary to have the introduction as they may never meet. However, don't forget that even the cat or dog that you have in your home loves to go out once in a while. The garden and the yard in your home is a space that your family pets love too. If you ignore the introduction, you may have to witness sudden and rather unpleasant ones!

The introduction should never be hurried. Make sure that the animals and birds have enough space and time to get used to each other. You must also be very careful to ensure that your chicken is completely protected.

When you are introducing your pet and the chicken for the first time, try to keep the bird in an enclosure. You may also tie your family pet up during the introduction. The last option is to hold the chicken in your arms during the introduction. Whatever you do, make sure that the introduction is fully supervised. Since you are not sure about the reaction, you must never take any chances.

If you have a pet cat at home, the most important thing to understand is that the garden is as much the cat's territory as it is the chicken's territory. Cats are naturally very curious and they tend to poke around in the garden. They are usually more interested in the rodents than the chickens. So the introduction of cats and chickens are a lot safer.

On the other hand, if you are trying to introduce your chicken to a dog, the precautions that you need to take are greater. It is always best that you introduce your pet dog to chickens when he is still a puppy. You see, there are some breeds of dogs that are "dog birds". These breeds love to chase birds around. Since the chicken is easier to catch in comparison to the other birds, the natural instinct may kick in, making it fatal for the chicken.

It is true that dogs are considered as suitable guardians to chickens. There are several families who will leave the dog alone with the chickens. This is alright when the chickens and dogs are in a garden setting where the chickens have enough space to escape if the dog becomes aggressive. However, there are also many tragic instances when entire flocks have been destroyed because the dog's instincts kick in.

It is definitely recommended that you be extremely protective with your chickens. At the same time, be patient with your canine friend. Always make sure that the introductions are in a protected environment. The chickens should be in an enclosed space till you know that the dog is used to their presence. The next step would be to directly introduce the two while the chicken in in your arms.

If your dog has been trained well, it is a bonus. If he can "heel" and "stay" at your command, your chickens are safer. You may also keep your dog on a leash when the chickens are free range. Once the chickens are not "new" or interesting to your dog, you can be more rest assured that he will be easily distracted by other things. Most often, dogs will find squirrels more interesting than the chickens that they see on a daily basis. So, if you want your pets to be at peace with each other, make sure that they spend plenty of time with each other.

Also, you must be open to the fact that some breeds are more aggressive than the others. So, even when you are introducing family pets over and over to the chickens, you cannot be sure that the chickens are entirely safe. Of course, they will get used to each other. However, whether they can really be the best of friends is an entirely different question.

The most tragic thing is knowing that your dog or cat can be harmful for your flock. In most cases, you will know that your dog or cat is harmful only after a fatality. In such cases, you will have to choose between your chicken and your existing pet. Of course, in most cases the pet that has been with an owner for longer gets preference. There is no reason to be upset with your family pet as the reaction is just the result of a very strong instinct.

5. Quarantine measures

The biggest threat with chickens is the possibility of infections due to Salmonella. There are several ways that these birds transmit Salmonella. If you are considering an indoor pet, especially, you must take additional quarantine measures to ensure the safety of your family.

How Salmonella is transmitted

Chickens usually carry salmonella on their bodies, within their plumes and on their feet. They will also release salmonella in their droppings. Therefore, people around the chickens are constantly in the danger of coming in touch with Salmonella.

These germs are not restricted to the body and feces of the bird. Everything that your chicken comes in contact with is infected. This includes the cage, the soil, the plants and even the clothing of people who handle the birds. So when someone unknowingly comes in contact with any of these elements in a chicken's environment, they are likely to be infected. The biggest problem arises when the hand or object that is infected with Salmonella reaches the area around the mouth.

Children are at maximum risk of infection as their immune system is not entirely developed. In addition to that, children have the tendency to put their fingers in their mouths. It is possible to avoid infections by taking simple measures.

The simplest thing to do is washing your hands every time you handle the chicken or come in contact with their immediate environment. This sounds quite doable for both adults and infants. However, there is one section of your family that is still in danger. Yes, I am talking about other chickens and pets that you have at home.

Sometimes, a new bird may have infections that will prove fatal to chickens and other fowl present in your farm or garden. The only way to overcome this is by taking adequate measures to quarantine.

Quarantining requires you to keep the new bird away from the rest of the birds for at least 2 to 3 weeks. During this period, your new bird will require a separate coop or house to ensure that he does not mingle with the birds. Many chicken owners neglect quarantining to avoid the expense of an additional coop. However, it is worth the investment considering that the entire existing flock is in danger of infection.

While your chicken is in quarantine, you must make sure that you give it highly nutritious foods. Giving them Vitamin tonics are also recommended to help take care of injuries, if any.

In case you have two separate flocks of birds, make sure you disinfect yourself while dealing with either group. This means that you must wash your hands thoroughly, change your clothes and even use separate equipment for these two groups. This will ensure that neither of them comes down with an infection that the other might have and actually be immune to!

6. The final checklist

When you are bringing home a new pet, there are so many things that you need to worry about that you might simply forget a few in all the excitement. This checklist is for all you beginners who are already fumbling with the right preparations to make your home a perfect place to raise healthy chickens in.

- Get permission from your local authorities
- Inform your neighbors
- Make enough space for the birds
- Prepare the coops
- Get comfortable and warm bedding
- Keep aside nesting boxes
- Prepare roosts
- Prepare feeders
- Place many waterers
- Keep manure boxes handy
- Keep the feed ready
- Make sure you have access to incubators
- Keep probe thermometers handy
- Storage containers
- Keep heaters for chicks
- Baskets for egg collection

We will discuss in greater detail about these supplies in the following chapters. When you are preparing your home for a chicken or a flock, make sure that you have everything that you need handy. This will make the transition and acclimatization easier for the bird. You will also feel less overwhelmed if you have everything in place to welcome your new birds. You will find all the supplies you need at local pet stores or even online.

Chapter 8: Housing Your Buff Orpington Chickens

The type of housing that you make for your chickens determines how safe and healthy they will be. One of the most important things to do when you bring home chickens is building a coop for them. Most people believe that pets like chickens are free range and hence do not require any sort of housing. You would even like to believe that it is best to leave them in an environment that is natural for them to thrive in. However, you could be completely mistaken.

There are several dangers out there that can seriously jeopardize the well-being of your flock. So, you must make sure that they have a safe environment to live in peacefully. So when you bring home chickens, you need to build proper housing facilities because:

-       Predators are always on the prowl. Since these chickens are flightless, they make very easy targets. They cannot escape by flying away from danger like other chickens in the wild.

-       Chickens are also capable of running away. If the space that they are kept in is not enclosed, they might wander away and be seriously injured.

-       Free range pets are most often killed by traffic. If your farm or home is close to a busy freeway, you must be additionally cautious when you bring home a chicken.

-       Chickens require a warm shelter at night to remain healthy. Chickens, in particular, love a calm and secluded place to roost at night. They may feel uncomfortable and even threatened if that does not happen.

There are several options when it comes to housing your chickens. You may either choose to build your own little coop or house or you may also bring in special chicken coops that are available in pet stores. There are several professionals who will be able to come to your home and install large coops if necessary.

1. Building the perfect coop

The coop is a place where the chicken will spend most of the day. This is where the chicken will lay its eggs, nest or even keep itself safe from bad weather. There are several types of coops that you can build for your chickens. You will be able to get ready to make coops in most pet stores and hardware stores. You can also rely on the Internet to make simple, yet sturdy chicken coops. The most important thing that you need to keep in mind is making the coops as safe and comfortable for the chicken as possible.

Here are some tips that will help you build the perfect coop for your beloved pet:

• Space is a very important issue when it comes to the chicken coop. As a thumb rule, you must at least allow four square feet for every chicken inside the coop. If you have Buff Orpington Chickens, 2 square feet per chicken is decent. The next thing is to provide ample outdoor space. For every large sized fowl, you need to provide at least 10 feet per bird. In case of Buff Orpington Chickens, you need to allow about 8 square feet per bird.

• If the coop is not well ventilated, the birds won't thrive well. At the same time, there should not be any drafts as the birds will not be able to keep themselves warm at night. The best way to ensure that you get the best of both worlds is to keep the airflow high while allowing the chickens to stay low when they are roosting. You must remember that chickens will increase the levels of moisture within the coop. The ammonia contained in their feces is also high. So if these elements are not vented out regularly, the repercussions can be serious.

• The perches in the coop should be removable. This will help you clean and disinfect them easily. You see, the perches are perfect breeding places for mites and parasites that can be extremely dangerous for the chickens.

• The coop should contain nesting boxes. This is a vital part of the coop as your hens will mostly spend their time in the coop when they are broody. Every box should be big enough to nest at least one large hen comfortably. This means that the box should be at least 30 cm square in size. Every nesting box will have a small lip at the end. The advantage of this lip is that it ensures that the eggs do not roll away. You can also add some pine needles, sawdust or straw on the floor of the nesting box to make it a little more absorbent.
- 	Make the nesting boxes dark
- 	Keep them in a place where you can access them easily from the outside.
• The floor of the coop is also very important. You must make sure that you use pine wood chips to line the floor well. Always avoid cedar chips as they may be extremely toxic to the chickens. You may also use straw as a flooring option. It is a good idea to place dropping boards inside the coop. That way, all the poop of your chicken can be cleaned easily.

• When you are building a coop, be sure that you are prepared for the entire year. There will be a hot season and a cold season that your chickens will have to go through. In the summer months, make sure that there is enough shade for the chickens. In the winter months, the option of a water heater or a heating lamp is extremely important for the chickens.

• Another concern with chickens is burrowing animals. If there are rats or mice, you must also protect the coops from them to ensure that the eggs are safe. For this, you can lay fencing wire around the coop. Bury it in the ground up to about 15 cms. If pests try to get into the coop by making a burrow, they will be blocked by the metal wires.

• Once the coop has been made completely, make sure you check it again. Any protruding wire or nail in the coop can cause serious injuries to the bird.

You see, building a safe coop is not rocket science. All you need to do is ensure that the birds are warm and safe while they have ample space to move around. In keeping this as the basic need for a coop, you can choose amongst the different types that are available. Chicken coops have been developed over the years to make them easily adaptable in the urban set up. With the changing needs of chicken owners, the designs of the coops have also changed.

When you are building a coop for your chicken, you must consider all the space and economic restrictions that you may face. When you have a budget in mind, you will be able to build a suitable coop for your feathered friends. You must also be aware of the ways in which you will utilise your coop. If you have only two or three chickens, you may want to have a coop that also serves as a portable carrier. On the other hand, when you have a large group of chickens in your home, the coop needs to be more manageable. Here are a few options that you can choose from.

2. Types of chicken coops

The utility and the budget of a coop determine the size and the type of the coop. You must make sure that you have clearly understood these factors before you actually have a coop installed in your home. There are several types of coops available for you to choose from. Here are the basic types of coops that are used these days:

A chicken ark

If you live in a place which is infested with predators, then you may use a chicken ark to keep your chickens. Chicken arks are perfect for conditions in which the chicken cannot be allowed to range freely due to safety considerations. You may also have pets or rogue animals from the neighbourhood that threaten the safety of your birds. In such cases, the ark is a perfect choice.

Chicken arks provide ample sunlight through meshed doors and windows. At the same time, they keep the chickens indoors and completely protected.

Another advantage with these arks is that they are portable. So, you can actually choose the spot in which your chickens will graze for the day. The ark is a simple overhead enclosure. The floor is usually absent. So when you change the location of the ark, the birds can still have the pleasure of scratching the ground and foraging for worms and insects.

So, if you ever feel guilty for not letting your chickens out in the open, all you need to do is build an ark on your own. In case you are not too good with woodwork, you can even hire professionals to help you with the ark for your pet chickens.

Chicken house

In the year 1895, a chicken house was designed by Tater Gate. It is also popularly known as the Mammy's Chicken house. This design is based on the coop designed by his grandparents.

The original coop that was built in Kentucky stands to this date. This is enough evidence for the fact that the chicken house was extremely sturdy. Therefore, it might as well be voted as the safest option to house your chickens.

The advantage with this type of coop is that while the chickens are well protected, the coop is really easy to maintain. The coop consists of solid wood walls and a strong meshed flooring.

The highlight of this design is the fenced run that allows the chickens to enjoy the great outdoors while staying clear of deadly predators. There are roosts and nesting boxes that make the coop warm. It also has retractable windows to ensure that there is ample ventilation.

The Poultry Shed

This is one of the easiest and the most economical options when it comes to housing chickens. In fact, even an amateur can build a poultry shed on his own. These sheds become portable and more efficient when they are built on skids. That allows you to move them wherever you need quite easily.

If the biggest threat to the safety of your flock is ground predators, you can also elevate the shed on piers. When the coop is on a pier, the contact with moisture is also reduced, making the ground last longer.

As for the ventilation options, you can make the poultry shed more airy by using pieces of fiberglass that can be easily removed during the warmer months. The windows may also have wooden sashes that will make it easy to control the ventilation inside the coop. Your coop will also have a finished look if you opt for the wooden sashes.

A poultry shed is always fully equipped. It is possible to install roosts, nests, waterers and feeders inside this shed to help create the perfect ambience for your chickens.

The size may be the only disappointing feature as you cannot house more than one dozen chickens each time.

3. Creating the perfect ambience

It is not enough to simply build a coop for your chickens. You need to make sure that the coop is utilised fully. This is possible only when the ambience within the coop is perfect for your flock to thrive in.

When you build a coop, you must equip it with everything that your chickens will require. Whether they are brooding or simply carrying out mundane daily activities, your coop must facilitate it completely. There are a few installations that you must make inside or around the coop in order to create the perfect ambience for your chickens. The three most essential things along with the coop are:

The Chicken Roost

A roost is the place where the chicken will go to sleep. This roost is always at a really high point. Most often chickens will roost together in a group in order to feel protected and warm when they are asleep.

This is their natural instinct and they will always perch on the highest point and fall asleep in the wild. As the owner, it is your job to make sure that this instinct is kept alive even in your pet chickens. Remember, when you play along with the natural instincts of your pets, they will be happier and will thrive better. So when you design the space that they will live in, having a roost is mandatory.

Never keep the roosts at different levels. You see, chickens are not really fond of "bunk beds". If they see that one roost is higher than the other, they will fight each other for the highest point available. So, all the roosts must be of the same height.

The chicken roost is really simple to create. It is merely a board or a wooden rod that you will install in the coop. If you want it to be really natural and rustic, you can also place a branch in the coop as a roost. All you need to make sure is that the dimensions are right. The roost must either be 2"X2" or 2"X4". In case you decide to use wooden planks, make sure that you round off the edges to avoid splinters.

When you are placing the roost in the coop, you must be aware of the processes that are part of a chicken's natural sleep cycle. You must know that a chicken will poop a lot when he is asleep. This piece if information is vital as it will help you decide where you want the maximum amount of poop to be collected. This will be as per your cleaning convenience.

The best place to mount the roost is in areas where you will not walk in order to collect the eggs. You also need to make sure that the roost is not near the nesting areas. You need to plan the placement of your roost well in advance as your job of managing the chickens will become much easier if you do so. If you are a cleanliness freak, you could also place a litter box right under the roost to collect all the poop. This makes it easier to clean the coop. When you add the poop and the flooring material of the coop to your garden, it can make great fertilizer. There are two thumb rules that you need to follow when you are building your roost:

- It should never be above the nesting area
- It should not be in the path that you walk in.

The length of the roost is also important. You must make sure that the chickens have enough place to rest peacefully. The ideal size for each roost would be about 10" in length.

If you are in the habit of clipping the wings of your chickens, you will have to add one more structure to make the roost accessible to the chickens. When the wings have been clipped, it renders the chicken completely flightless. So, you will have to add a small ladder that the chicken can climb up to reach the roost. If you have watched closely, this tiny ladder is present in most coops these days.

Waterer

You must ensure that chickens are never fed without water. Many chicken owners have a misconception that chickens may drink too much water and actually die. Hence they keep the waterers away from the chickens while feeding them.

This practice is never recommended as chickens require water more than food. Especially when you are feeding the chickens dry pellets, you must make sure that you provide water alongside. When chickens eat dry pellets or crumbs and fail to have an adequate amount of water, the feed begins to swell inside the chicken. The risk of choking is also high when chickens are given dry food without water.

So, make sure that you always have enough clean drinking water for the chickens.

Feeders

The biggest challenge with chickens is to monitor their feed and to makes sure that they eat regularly. If you are not able to do this hands on, you can use a food dispenser that works quite well.

The most basic type of food dispenser consists of a plastic dome like structure that has a roof to keep the food dry. It has a small feeder around it where the chickens can eat. The beauty of this dispenser is that it keeps refilling the feeder as the chickens finish eating. So, all you need to do is fill the dispenser regularly and be care free.

Another interesting type of food dispenser is the tread plate feeder. With this type of feeder, a small metal tread plate provides access to the food. Every time a chicken steps on this feeder, it will open the lid to the container which stores the bird feed.

An automatic pet feeder is only useful when you have smaller flocks of chickens. These feeders are ideal to feed one or two pets each time. So if you have between 2 to 4 chickens, this type of feeder might work well for you.

Automatic pet feeders have been designed for people who are unable to stay at home all day to ensure that their pets are being fed on time. It is possible to program close to 10 meals each day for your Chicken. You can set the program to dispense an exact amount of bird feed each time. You also have the option of setting different portions each time.

You can time these automatic feeders and be assured that your pet chickens will not remain hungry. Like I mentioned before, chickens are not really dependent on their owners for their food. They can easily forage for their food. In case you have to keep your chickens indoor for some reason, this type of feeder works best. For instance, if your chicken has undergone any surgery or is under treatment, he may not be able to forage. In such cases an automatic dispenser works best.

Besides making your life easier, food dispensers serve several other purposes. Now, birds have very tiny digestive tracts. That's why they poop so often. Undoubtedly, they also remain hungry all the time and constantly require food. With a food dispenser you can ensure that your precious pets have access to food all the time.

A common problem that most chicken owners face is finding poop in the food very often. Using a food dispenser puts an end to this rather difficult problem. Also, you will not have to deal with upturned bowls of food. This reduces wastage and ensures that the food is stored in hygienic conditions.

4. Bedding options for Chickens

The bedding that you place in the coops should be made from a material that will be able to keep the chickens warm and dry throughout. It must also be easy to clean. If the material that you are using has the property of retaining water, then you will notice that it will be very hard to maintain the coop well. So, for best results, you must use the following bedding options in your coop:

Pine Shavings: This is the most preferred type of bedding option as chickens simply love it. It is ideal for smaller flocks. The best thing about pine shavings is that they are highly absorbent. They have the ability to soak in not only the wetness but also the odor of the poop. They help you manage the litter well. Additionally, pine shavings are also very soft and light. So, even if the hens lay eggs on this type of bedding, the eggs will not be damaged. The shavings are extremely easy to replace. They are also highly affordable and easily available. If you are buying pine shavings online, make sure you don't get confused between chips and shavings. Pine chips are terrible bedding options.

Straw and Hay: This is a popular bedding choice among people who have small farms. The reason that it is so popular is that it is extremely affordable and really durable. It is also a good absorbent that has the ability to soak the wetness and also soak the odor. The quality of the straw and hay is important. If you compromise on this, the straw will remain moist, making the coop smell really bad.

Shredded Paper: In case you run out of your regular bedding material, shredded paper can make a great alternative. It is also considered one of the most popular trends among chicken owners. This is not only a good bedding option but is also a great way to recycle paper. The best thing is that you will never run out of it. All you need to do is shred the newspaper in your home into small pieces and lay it on the floor neatly. Newspaper shredding is a great absorbent like any other bedding material. The chickens will not be harmed by it at all.

Sand: Sand is a really interesting option for coop bedding. The first and the most important thing is that sand is completely natural. Hence, it will not harm the birds even a little. Sand along with the bird poop can make great compost. Of course, sand will also give the chicken an opportunity to scratch and, well, be chickens!

Sawdust: This is a rather novel idea in the world of chicken keeping. Sawdust is great as it is really soft. So the eggs that are laid will not be damaged. Sawdust also has a natural smell that keeps the coop fresh all day long. During the colder months, sawdust makes a great bedding option as it can be really warm. The only disadvantage with sawdust is that it retains water. It is also prone to bacteria. So, you must make sure that you change the sawdust regularly if you choose to use it.

When you are choosing the bedding option for the coop, there is one more thing that you must consider. If your chickens are sharing the coop with other birds, you must avoid bedding that will not suit the other bird.

5. Keeping predators at bay

The biggest problem with having chickens in your garden is the danger of predators. It is heart-breaking when you realize that one of your beauties has been taken away or killed by a predatory animal. Of course, this is a natural process that you cannot really stop. What you can do is keep your Chickens in enclosures when you are not around to supervise, especially at night. You can also build fences to keep the predators away from your chickens.

The difficult part is that chickens are usually extremely vulnerable when they are domesticated. So, they become easy prey for animals like coyotes, foxes, bobcats and raccoons. With animals like the coyote, you can even expect attacks in broad daylight. So you must take several preventive measures to ensure that your Chickens are safe. Some methods you can use are:

- Allow your chickens out in the open. This is required for them to survive. However, if you have noticed attacks during the day, make sure you have someone to supervise the birds.

- Get rid of possible hiding spots for predators. Coyotes, especially, love hiding in thick bushes before attacking the chickens.

- Getting a dog will help if your predator problem is coming from bobcats. They are effective against other animals, too. However, bob cats can be kept at bay only with dogs as no fence or enclosure will stop them.

- Direct your chickens into enclosures every night. They are difficult to pen. However, you can lure them with treats and certain sounds to make sure that they get into their enclosures at night.

- Use fences as the primary defense against predators.

- Do not leave garbage out in the open. Usually, predators like raccoons are first attracted by the smell of the garbage. If you can keep your space clean, you can avoid such animals.

If you think that predators are a serious problem, you may also contact your Environment Protection Council. They will be able to give you more definite methods to keep predators away. If the problem still persists, keeping the chickens in spacious coops or chicken tractors is the best option. You can create the right environment for the chickens within this environment so that they continue to forage and have a good time.

The best way to control predators is to use fencing around your home. There are several fencing options that can be used. Some of them can also be used to direct and control your flocks.

6. Fencing options

Temporary Fencing

Temporary fencing serves two purposes. It can be used to separate various farm animals and can also be used to direct them into their enclosures. The primary function of a temporary or portable fence is to mark boundaries and actually control your animal groups.

The most common type of temporary fence is the chain link fence. You can get long rolls of chain links that are arranged in a zigzag pattern. The heavy base allows you to place them where you need. Another simple type of temporary fencing is the mesh fence. It is similar to the chain link fence but is more secure as the base is heavier.

If you need to keep out larger farm animals like dogs or sheep, you can use a picket fence. They have vertically arranged wires that have a very strong base to keep these animals away from your poultry.

Chicken wires or poultry fences are the most common type of temporary fences used to keep chickens separate. These fences are ready to install and can be adjusted as per your needs. They do not require any tools for installation and work perfectly well on all terrains.

Permanent Fencing

Permanent fences do not serve the purpose of separating different farm animals. They are used to mark the boundary of your garden to prevent animals from getting out or getting in to your property. For instance, if you have a freeway near your home, a permanent fence will keep your chickens from getting away from your garden or farm. They also keep predators at bay.

Needless to say, these structures, once installed must not be removed. They must also be able to keep small animals and birds from getting in and out. In addition to that, they must also be strong enough to hold on for several years.

The most common type of permanent fencing used to keep your Chickens Safe is the wooden or bamboo fencing. Panels of wood and bamboo are installed around the perimeter of your space. You must make sure that there are no gaps in between panels. Concrete fences are also used. They are sturdier and are also great at keeping predators away.

Electric fences are not my favourite option. Of course, many blogs and websites suggest them as an effective way to keep predators away. However, there are chances that your own pets will get electrocuted. Of course, it is a cruel option whether you are thinking of keeping predators or pets in their boundaries.

Chapter 9: Daily Care For Buff Orpington Chickens

Like I have maintained throughout this book, keeping Buff Orpington Chickens at home is a lot of responsibility. Each day, you will have to dedicate at least 40 mins to 1 hour to taking care of your chickens. There are also several semi-annual and annual activities that are a part of chicken care. You must be able to carry them all out. If not, you are not ready to own a chicken.

1. Feeding Buff Orpington Chickens

The first thing that you need to do when you bring home your Buff Orpington Chickens or chicks is keep plenty of food available for them to eat. Chickens have specific nutritional requirements at different stages of their lives. So, depending upon whether you have chicks, brooders or chickens, you need to change the diet that you have set on a regular basis.

Feeding baby chicks

If you have just brought home baby chicks or if you have just hatched some eggs in your home, you might be a little sceptical about the food that you give your baby chicks. To begin with you can give them some crumbles and mash. These foods are specially formulated to enhance the growth of your chicks. If you have layer foods in your stock, make sure you never feed it to the chicks. Even in an emergency, you will not give your chicks this as it is high in calcium content that may be fatal to the delicate little chicks.

In case of a real emergency, you can give your chicks a blend of cornmeal and oats. Just run them for one round in the blender and when they have reached the crumble consistency, you can feed them to the chicks. You can use emergency feed for only one day as you must ensure that the chicks have a healthy and nutritious diet.

The food that you give your chicks should never have more than 21% proteins. In case the protein content is too high, the growth of the chicks becomes stunted. In the first few days, all you need to do is sprinkle the food on a towel so that the chicks actually learn to eat. Only when you know that they are eating well should you switch to feeders. Starting them off with feeders might leave the coop in a mess. If it is not cleaned for a long time, there are chances that the coop will also get extremely contaminated.

Chicks will not be able to break the food in their mouths as they have no teeth. So the food that you provide them with should contain some material that will grind the food. This hard material, usually in the form of small rocks, is known as grit. With chicks, you must never use calcium rich grit like oyster shells. When you are using store bought grit, make sure that it has no traces of oyster shell. It is possible to make grit at home with decomposed granite. Just wash the granite and remove the sand that is present. Once you have dried the granite pieces, they can be provided as grit for your chicks. All you need in case of chicks is provide them with the basic nutrition. You will not have to do anything extra for your chickens to grow healthily.

Feeding adult chickens

The nutritional requirements for adult chickens is, undoubtedly, very different from that of the chicks. It is very important to ensure that the chicks are getting proper nutrition in order to maintain their health. If you neglect the feeding aspect of your daily care, be prepared for a number of diseases that can be fatal to your chickens. In extreme cases, it can take down the entire flock.

If you want to save a little on the chicken feed, you also have the option of making your own feed at home. Here are the ingredients that you will need when you are making chicken food at home:

- Split peas: Good source of proteins
- Lentils: Good source of proteins
- Oatmeal: In the form of rolled oats
- Barley: hulled barley keeps the intestines protected
- Sesame seeds: Good source of vitamin E and B
- Sunflower seeds: Promotes cardiac development of the chicks
- Flax Seeds: Good source of omega 3
- Winter wheat: Good source of gluten protein
- Corn: Energizing for the flock
- Quinoa: Good Source or dietary fibres
- Soft white wheat: Good source of carbohydrates
- Kelp granules: Good source of fiber, iron and potassium
- Granite grit: Helps in digestion
- Millet: Good source of proteins and carbohydrates along with other nutrients like phosphorous.
- Kamut: Provides energy for the flock.

You must mix equal portions of all the ingredients. Only the corn, soft white wheat and winter wheat must be increased to two and three portions respectively. Store them in an airtight container to keep them fresh.

Grit for the chickens

The most important part of the feed is the grit. Since the chickens do not have any teeth, the food needs to be broken down in some way to make it easier for them to digest. That is the role of the grit that you use in your chicken feed. There are two types of grit that are commercially available:

Flint grit or insoluble grit: This type of grit passes through the stomach or the gizzard of your chicken. There, the food is broken down completely and digested easily. When you are using flint grit, make sure that the size is correct. If the grit is too small, chances are that it will not do anything and just pass through the bird's stomach. So, if you are commercially purchasing the grit, make sure that you buy one that is suitable for the age of your birds.

If you allow your chickens to free range, they will also pick up a lot of grit while foraging through your garden. They will be able to find this grit on their own and will require very little help from you. However, if you are worried about predators attacking your chickens, you might opt to buy the grit yourself.

Flint grit is a little expensive. However, you will be able to buy it in large lots that will last for longer lengths of time. So, in order to aid proper digestion of food, it is a worthwhile investment.

Soluble grit

This type of grit is usually made from oyster shells. The other materials used to make soluble grit are limestone and cockle sells. This type of grit is used to provide a high amount of calcium for the bird. So it is mostly used to feed birds that are about to lay eggs. Some breeders also use ground egg shells as grit to provide enough calcium. I personally do not recommend this as it may promote the egg eating habit among the brooders.

Oyster shell grit or soluble grit is usually larger than the flint grit. It simply dissolves in the digestive system and is absorbed by the body of the chicken as a good source of calcium. This helps produce good quality shells and will also improve the bone health of the birds.

Food Options for Chickens

If you own a chicken, the first question that you must ask yourself is what do you feed them? Many pet owners make the blunder of feeding their chicken bread crumbs. If you are concerned about the nutrition of your chickens, you must make sure that the food is appropriate for their age as well as the time of the year.

• Natural Foods: Usually, chickens will forage for their food. Their natural diet includes several worms, insects and slugs. They also feed on grass. When you allow your chicken to obtain natural foods, you will see that the plumage is glossy and the beak has a rich color.

• Wheat: Wheat is a great source of nutrition for chickens that are approximately 5 weeks old. You must give the chickens a portion of grit along with the wheat. Now, like most birds, chickens are unable to chew their food. So they usually consume their foods with tine rocks and pellets that help digest the food better. This roughage that the chicken consumes is called grit and is very important when you provide chickens with foods like wheat. When your chickens are about 10 weeks old, you can put them on a diet which consists of 50% dry pellets and 50% wheat.

• Commercial pellets: There are several brands of commercial hen pellets that are available in the market. You can simply pick up the right one based on the age and the nutritional requirements of your flock. These pellets are usually designed for the productive eggs. If you are choosing to give your hens pellets, you will have to make sure that it makes up the bigger chunk of your flock's feed. Ensure that the chickens have access to these pellets all day long. When a chicken is going to roost, he must do so with a full tummy. This is especially true for layers. Usually, the formation of the egg takes about 25 hours. When the hens are asleep, the egg is still building inside. The raw material that is required to build the egg is obtained from the food that she is digesting. So, never restrict the food source for your flock.

• Table Scraps: This is something that chickens absolutely love! Your pet chickens will appreciate anything from coffee beans to toast. Sometimes they may not eat certain food due to personal preferences. Of course, not all these foods are ideal for your chicken. If you do want to feed your chickens kitchen scraps, assign a special feeder. Simply throwing it into the chicken run will result in one colossal mess!

Medicated Feed

Medicated feed is usually given to birds that are prone to diseases and parasites. Usually, medicated feed is given to turkeys and chickens more often. However, with the understanding of common domestic fowl disease, medicated feed has been extended to chickens as well.

The most common diseases with chickens include colibacillosis, salmonellosis and fowl cholera. Salmonellosis and fowl cholera is also caused by bacterial infections. These diseases cause a lot of weakness in the chickens and can, in many cases, result in the death of the chicken. It is important to manage and control these diseases by providing the chickens with the right kind of food.

The use of medicated feed has been quite useful in several cases. However, only this is not good enough for 100% disease prevention. You must ensure that you maintain the right standards of hygiene and sanitation to keep the chickens healthy.

Supplements for Chickens

Chickens require a high protein diet to be healthy. At the same time, the balance in these nutrients also needs to be maintained. If the chicken has excess proteins in its diet, you will notice that the feathers will start bending upwards.

Besides proteins, calcium and phosphorous also form an important part of the diet. The quality of the egg depends entirely upon the calcium consumed by the chickens. In case they are laying eggs with very thin shells, it is an indication that they are not getting enough calcium and phosphorous.

Another important nutrient required for Buff Orpington Chickens is Niacin. This vitamin is essential in the correct development of the chicken's legs. If you notice that the chicken is not finding enough strength in its legs or is unable to walk properly, it could be a sign of niacin deficiency.

To make up for these deficiencies, you can use supplements that are readily available on the market. Usually, these supplements are available in the form of tablets in all pet stores.

However, when you are buying supplements for your chicken, make sure you consult your veterinarian. Only when they are prescribed should you include supplements in the diet of your chickens. Even an overdose of nutrients may have adverse effects. Therefore, you must be extremely cautious.

Nutritional Concern for laying chickens

When your chickens are breeding and ready to lay eggs, the kind of nutrition that they require is entirely different. The food that they eat needs to be nutritious enough to ensure that the eggs are healthy.

For this, you must give them something called layers pellets. These pellets are special as they have excess calcium and phosphorous. Usually, the best time to feed the chicken layering pellets is at the end of the day. You must make sure that you get special layers pellets designed for chickens. Most owners will simply feed their chickens layers pellets meant for hens. These pellets contain too much calcium and also have additional substances like egg yolk colors. To make the meal wholesome for the chicken that is lying, you can mix these pellets with an equal portion of wheat.

You can make out when a chicken is ready to lay eggs when the abdomen looks fuller than usual. It is best to start providing layer pellets from the months of February as the eggs are most likely to be laid in the summer months.

The quality of the food that you provide to the chickens should be noted very carefully. Remember, a certain brand of pellet that is more expensive than the others available in the market will contain a higher concentration of vitamins A, D and E. Avoid purchasing maintenance pellets.

For your chickens to breed, the correct diet is important. It is only when you take care of the nutrition of these chickens that the embryos will be healthy. If your chicken is able to obtain free range food safely, it is also a great option when they are ready to lay eggs.

What not to feed them

Of course, like all pets, even chickens can be harmed by feeding them certain things. Many breeders and vets will encourage you to feed your bird with table scraps. Of course, that is alright as long as you know what you are putting into the tummy of your bird.

Pet owners often get so attached to their pets that they begin to treat them like they are part of the family. Yes, that is a good thing as long as you do not treat your pet like humans, in the anatomic sense. You see, the digestive tract of your chicken is not designed to process all the foods that you consume. So, some things that you might consider extremely healthy for your family can actually ruin the health of your chicken. In some cases, it may even kill your bird.

Here are some foods that you must avoid entirely when it comes to domestic fowl:

- Uncooked Rice
- Alcoholic beverages
- Mushrooms

- Avocadoes
- Energy Drinks
- Lettuce
- Grapefruit
- Tomatoes
- Tea
- Coffee or other caffeine containing foods
- Cabbage
- High sugar foods
- Spinach and other foods high in oxalic acid
- Tobacco
- Cigarettes
- Garlic
- Peanuts
- Processed and Salted foods
- Lollies
- Parsley
- Leeks
- Aloe Vera
- Bamboo Shoots
- Fruits belonging to the prunus species
- Other pet foods
- Figs
- Chamomile
- Celery

These foods must always be avoided to ensure that your chickens are healthy and developing properly.

2. Keeping the coop clean

Infections are always on the prowl when it comes to your chickens. These birds tend to create a lot of moisture in the coops. As a result, they also attract bacteria and parasites that can cause serious damage to their health.

As the owner, it is your responsibility to ensure that your chickens are kept in healthy and clean conditions at all times. The process of cleaning the chicken coop can be tedious. However, if you are able to assign a special day and dedicate some time to doing this properly, you should not have too many issues with the cleaning. I will break down the coop cleaning process into a few simple steps that will make it less overwhelming for you:

Step 1: Get a good cleaning agent

There are several coop cleaners available in super markets and in pet stores. While most people simply use regular detergents for the coops, I suggest that you use the ones that are meant specifically for coop maintenance. The thing with regular detergents is that they may contain several chemicals that may be harmful for the flock.

Chickens are prone to infections, respiratory diseases and also skin problems. So, using cleaners that are full of toxins can never be the best idea. There are several natural options for coop cleaning. I like to use a white vinegar based cleaner. This is not only effective in cleaning the coop but is also extremely gentle and mild on the chickens.

It is a little bit of preparation; however, since the health of the chickens is priority, it is worth all the effort. If you have scheduled the coop cleaning day, you must make this white vinegar cleaner at least a month in advance. It takes that much time to prepare the solution properly.

In order to make the cleaner, you will need the peel of four oranges, two cinnamon sticks, vanilla beans and white vinegar. You need to also have canning jars to brew the cleaner in. Divide the ingredients into two portions and place them in the canning jars. Then pour the white vinegar over these ingredients. Tighten the jars and keep the solution aside for about a month. Make sure you shake the mixture occasionally for best results. The advantage with this type of cleaner is that it will kill mold, repel the insects and also keep the coop smelling clean.

Step 2: Get all your supplies

The last thing you want to do when you are cleaning the coop is run back and forth to get your supplies. So here is a checklist that will help you ensure that you have everything that you need when you begin to clean your coop:

- A large bucket to collect the dirt
- Cleaning brushes
- Duster
- Spray bottle for the cleaner
- Detergent, if you are using any
- Rubber gloves
- A mask if you are allergic to chicken droppings
- A small pail
- Litter or bedding

Step 3: Get the chickens out

Of course, this is an important step. This is when you will realise that having a portable coop is also necessary when you are raising chickens. Even having a temporary fencing option is great as far as the chickens are concerned. You must pick all the chickens out and place them in the coop or in the fencing before you begin. This will help you have access to the entire coop for cleaning.

If your flock is already laying eggs, be sure to collect the eggs before you begin to clean the coop. Having eggs in the coop when you start cleaning can lead to unwanted breakage and destruction of the eggs.

Step 4: Scrub it out

Once your chickens and eggs are out of the coop, the only thing that is left to do is clean the space thoroughly. Wear your rubber gloves and get started with the litter. Rake the litter out and collect it in the large bucket. Remember that the litter can make great manure for your garden.

The next thing to do would be to get all the roosts out of the way. Take them out and place them in some sunshine. That will help get rid of the smell and also the droppings. Once the roost has been aired well, you can simple scrape off the droppings if any.

Make sure you air out the entire coop. This means that you open all the doors and the ventilators to let the fresh air in. Since coops are usually closed to prevent drafts, the smell can remain locked in for long periods of time. This is not pleasant when you are in the coop trying to clean it.

The next thing is to get down to the dirty business. You will have to scrub your coop clean. Use the cleaner that you have made to remove all the stains and dirt from the floor of the coop. In case you are using a detergent, you will have to thoroughly dry the coop before you let the chickens in. Paying a little extra and getting linoleum flooring for the coop can really help make the cleaning process much easier. You must also wipe down the windows and the doors to give the coop a thorough cleaner.

When the coop is dry, you can use a special poultry protector spray. This spray keeps the infections and the bacteria at bay. You will be able to get this special solution in most pet stores or super markets. You can also do a special pest controlling method to cleanse the coop thoroughly. You can use food grade diatomaceous earth on the floor, the roosts and all the nooks of your coop.

Step 5: The final touches

Once you have thoroughly cleaned and disinfected the entire coop, you can replace the bedding or the litter. Simply rake in the new litter on the floor of the coop.
Another nice touch you can add is a bit of fragrance. Use herbs like lavender or lemongrass for this. All you need to do is pluck out a few leaves and place them in the nesting boxes. This will help keep the coop smelling fresh all day long.

Making cleaning easier

I have always believed in making pet care easy so that you have time to actually enjoy having your pets around. If you feel like taking care of them is a hassle, it is quite sad, really. The one thing that most pet owners dread when it comes to their chickens is cleaning the coop. In order to simplify this process, I will give you a few tips that will be really handy for you:

• **Use dropping boxes/ boards:** If you are able to clean the dropping boxes regularly, it is good enough. You really do not have to worry about the floor getting messy with dried up poop that you have to scrub out with all your might. You can even use disposable dropping boxes that can simply be thrown away when they are too dirty.

• **Change the flooring:** Use a flooring material such as linoleum. This is easy to clean. Additionally, it will also not retain much moisture, making your job easier. All you need to do is mop it down once to leave it completely clean. If the floor is made of materials like wood, be prepared for moisture retention, moss, foul odor etc.

• **Make the roost removable:** The roost is where most of the dropping accumulates. The roost can be really difficult to clean as they are placed at certain heights that are not easily accessible. If you have roosts that are removable, all you have to do is take them out and air them for a while for best results.

• **Sand is your savior:** Undoubtedly, sand is the best litter or bedding option as far as cleaning goes. All you need to do is rake the sand out and your coop will be good as new. Sand also has the property of trapping the odor and not letting it spread all over the coop.

How often do you clean your coop

The cleaning frequency varies from one month to 2 weeks depending upon the size of the coop and the number of chickens that you have. If the coop is large enough for your chickens, cleaning is less frequent and is also a lot easier.

3. Grooming the chicken

Grooming your pet chickens is important especially if you plan to showcase them in exhibitions. If your chickens are staying indoors, you will have to clean and groom them on a regular basis to make sure that they are hygienic. Grooming a chicken can be quite a task if you are unsure of what you are doing. On the other hand, if you take your time and do it correctly, you will be surprised at how easy it actually is. In addition to that, your chickens will also enjoy a good bath.

If you are planning to show your chickens, you must bathe them at least 3 to 5 days before the show. This will give your bird plenty of time to dry up completely. The natural oils that are secreted by the skin of the bird will also come back on to the feathers making them shine. The process of grooming begins with clipping the nails and also trimming the beak before you give your chicken a bath. There are several last minute touch ups that you can do to keep your bird looking really good for the show.

Supplies you need

When it comes to bathing chickens, the supplies required are quite basic actually. Here is a list of things that you will need for your chickens:

- Large Washtubs: 3
- Vinegar
- Shampoo
- Small Sponge
- A carrier
- Toothbrush
- Pet nail clippers
- A blow drier
- Towels

- Conditioner

You can also keep an emery board handy to stop any bleeding during the clipping. You can also trim the beak and give it a nice shine using the emery board. Make sure that you gather all the supplies when you begin. They should be within your reach so that you can give your chickens a good bath in peace.

Giving your chicken a bath

Bathing the chickens is not as hard as most people make it out to be. All you need to do is keep it methodical. Here are the basic steps for bathing your chickens properly:

- Fill three large tubs with warm water. Make sure that the tubs are large enough for the birds. If they are too small, you will end up making a mess. The first tub is for the actual bath while the other two are to rinse the bird. The laundry room is my favourite place to do the messy job of washing my birds. In the first tub, add vinegar. You need to add a quarter cup for every gallon. The next tub will have a spoon of hair conditioner. The last tub will have plain water.

- You need to hold your chicken properly to keep it calm while you are giving it a bath. The best way to hold a chicken is with its chest resting on your palm. Gently release the bird into the tub and hold it firmly so that it can understand what is going on. Most often, chickens will relax after a few seconds. Sometimes, they will even fall asleep when you are giving them a bath. While this is adorable, you need to make sure that the head stays above the water at all times.

- When you are shampooing the bird, start with the dirtiest part of the bird. The areas that need maximum cleaning are the legs and the feet. You need to start with them so that the dirty parts can soak in the shampoo while you clean the rest of the bird. When you are shampooing the body of the bird, make sure you do not rub the feathers backwards.

91

• Take time to clean the bird thoroughly. When you feel like all the nooks and crannies have been shampooed well, it is time to rinse your bird. Rinse out as much shampoo as possible in the first tub itself. After that, place the bird in the second tub with the conditioner. Rinse well. Make sure that there is no shampoo on the feathers. Even the slightest bit of shampoo means that the feathers will be a mess when you try to dry them.

• The next step is to dry your chicken. Take it out of the water and roll it with a towel. Let the legs and the head stick out. Think of it like making an egg roll with your chicken! This way of drying the chicken will keep it still when you are wiping the feathers.

• Keeping the chicken wrapped in the towel, wash the face, the combs and the wattle. You can even trim the beak with the emery board when the chicken is held still in the wrap.

• Once you are done with the bathing, you need to give your beautiful Buff Orpington Chicken a good pedicure. You start by scrubbing the feet with the toothbrush. There may be a lot of dirt under the toe nails. They need to be scrubbed well and removed. You may also have to use some soap to do this properly.

• Clip the nails to finish off the grooming process. Use a regular pet nail clipper for this. After you have bathed your chicken, it is much easier as the nails will be soft and easy to clip. Just make sure that you do not clip the nails too short. If you clip the veins, the nails will begin to bleed. The blood will also get on to the feathers, destroying all your cleaning efforts. If your bird has white toe nails, it is relatively easy to see the toe nails. On the other hand, it the toenails are dark, you will have to look under the nails to see the toe nails. In case the nail starts to bleed, you can use cotton to stop the bleeding.

Now it is time to let the bird relax. Place it in a carrier and allow it to dry. You can also place the carrier in a clean corner of your home that receives a lot of sunlight. This will help keep your bird warm as it is drying off. Even after cleaning the bird thoroughly, there is some last minute grooming that you will have to do if you are taking your bird for a show.

4. Show grooming

When you are showing your chicken you need to do some last minute grooming that will take care of tiny specks of dirt on the body, feet or the beaks. It will also help you keep the feathers glossy and neat. In order to complete these grooming activities quickly it is a good idea to prepare a grooming box that consists of all the necessary supplies. Here is a list of things that you will need to put in the grooming box:

- Baby oil for the feet, shank, comb and beak
- A good blood stop
- Old toothbrush to clean the nails
- Wet wipes
- Antibiotic ointment for any wounds on the body
- Silk cloth to clean the feathers and make them shine

It is advised that you keep a separate grooming box with all the supplies that you need in the vehicle that you use to transport your chicken.

Grooming before the show

- It is best to keep the bird in a coop or a cage while you are waiting at the exhibition.
- When you know that you have about 30 minutes before the judgement process begins start grooming the bird.
- Begin with the feet and legs as they tend to get really dirty. Just wipe the legs with baby wipes and add some baby oil to give it some shine.

- The vent area needs to be checked for any dirt that might have accumulated on the feathers. If you find anything just wipe it off with the baby wipes.
- Check the head properly. If it seems dull you can add some baby oil on the wattles and the comb. These parts are most prone to injuries so you may also need to add some antibiotic cream. Whether you use baby oil or an ointment you need to rub it really well to ensure that you give it a good shine.

- Now rub the body of the bird from the head to its tail using the silk cloth. Rubbing it over 50 times is best recommended to give it a good shine. This also has another purpose. Rubbing the body will really calm the bird down and it will make it easier to present it to the judges.

You can pick up several techniques of cleaning and grooming the bird by watching different breeders and pet owners. You will also be able to understand what products work best for your bird as you gain more experience with showing and exhibitions.

5. The daily care checklist

Daily care for chickens must be extremely methodical. Forgetting even the slightest detail can affect the health of your chickens. So to make it easier for first time pet owners here is a quick checklist that you can use.

Checking the chickens

- Count your chicken every day.
- Do they look well or are they slow and lethargic?
- Do they sleep the right way?
- Do they seem anxious or scared?
- Is their crop appearing messy?
- Is the poop abnormal?

Checking the chicken poop

- Has the door been tampered with?

- Can you see signs of shoe marks or scratches on the poop?
- Can you see any loose slats that may fall off easily?
- Do you see droppings of other bird or animal besides the chicken?
- Do you see any signs of red mite invasion?
- Are there any leaks?
- Is the ventilation okay?
- Is the floor area secured?
- Is the water clean?
- Is the feeder full?

Checking the chicken run

- Can you see signs of a fox trying to dig in?
- Do you see fox droppings around the pen?
- Are there any branches that the fox could jump in from?
- Is the fencing completely secure?
- Have you shut the gate?
- Is there any place for the chicken to get out?

These pointers are extremely important as they put the chickens at risk. Keeping the door or the gate open is the cause for most deaths in a flock. It is very easy for predators to make their way into your home and harm the birds.

I cannot state with complete confidence that these are the only precautions you need to take. There are several reasons why chickens fall sick or even get eaten by predators. As the chicken owner you need to be extremely vigilant if there is even single death in your flock. Put in all the efforts possible to find out the reason for fatalities to ensure that it does not extend to the rest of the flock.

6. Seasonal care for chickens

Depending on the weather conditions and the temperatures in your area the kind of care you will take will vary greatly. The requirements of a bird are different in hotter months and different in the cooler months. Here are some things that you need to take care of during the summer and winter months respectively.

Summer care for chickens

The first thing that you need to take care of in the hotter months is the placement of your chicken coops. Usually a coop or a chicken tractor is placed in the middle of a garden. This gives them the opportunity to scratch around and forage the grass. However, as it gets hotter here are some things that you need to follow:

• The pen or coop should be placed near a hedge. This creates a comfortable environment for the birds as there is ample shade. If you let the bird range freely you will notice that their favourite spots are around the hedges and the bushes.
• In case the coops are not portable try to keep them covered.
• Keep the hen house closed at night. Make sure that there is enough ventilation to keep it airy and cool.
• If you see that the chicken is squatting strangely with its wings up in the air it means that the coop is too warm. That is your sign to increase ventilation and cooling.

Having a broody hen in the summer months is extremely worrying as the conditions that they live in should be near perfect. You see, a broody hen will spend most of its time in the nesting box. In the hotter months this can lead to dehydration. So you must make it a point to occasionally lift the chicken and take her to the water source. Always ensure that she has lots of water and a good source of fresh air.

In case you need to stay out for long hours during the hotter months build a separate shelter for the brooding hens. You must keep them in a separate fence area when you are not around. Just shutting the door of the coop is not good enough, as the other members of the flock will bully her.

During the summer months placing dust baths can be a great idea. These baths get nice and warm and make perfect resting places for the chickens. You will notice that the bird will spend several hours just lying in the dust bath flicking the wings once in a while. If you have a green house in your farm keep it open, as the hens love to rest there.

The good news about summer is maintenance is much easier than a winter month. Cleaning the coop is just $1/3^{rd}$ the work that is required than the colder months. The only thing you need to worry about during the hot months is the mite issues. So make sure that you inspect the coops regularly and check every nook and cranny. In case you witness any mites just use an eco-friendly powder that can be sprinkled in the areas that are infected to keep the coop clean.

Winter care for chickens

Usually in the winter months most chicken owners tend to keep lights in the chicken house. This method does not serve the purpose keeping your chickens warm. The only thing it does is increase the daylight hours for your hens. This artificial daylight promotes more egg laying. However, using lights in the coop will reduce the egg laying life of the hen eventually. If you observe most of the commercial egg farms, artificial lights are introduced only for chickens that are ready to be slaughtered after a year.

Additionally, the lights that are used in the farms are tiny. They will come on early in the mornings and will go off at night. This timer will create the effect of a regular sunrise and will not alter the body clock of the chicken much.

The maintenance of the coop is quite harder during the winter months. As I mentioned before, chickens tend to poop the most when they are roosting in the dark. Since the dark hours are longer in the winter months chickens tend to remain on the roosts. This increases the poop that they produce. So the cleaning of the coop is almost doubled in the winter months. Security is another issue in the winter months as the foxes have fewer natural sources to obtain their food. This makes them more interested in your coops. So be on the lookout for any signs that show a predator on the prowl.

Chapter 10: Interacting With The Chickens

1. Handling Baby Chickens

During the process of raising young chickens, it will often be necessary to move them from one place to another. Fortunately, for the first few months of their lives, chickens can be held without great difficulty. They may still defecate when lifted off the ground, but because they are small, it is easier to keep the "yucky end" pointed away from you.

Young chickens may peck at the hand that holds them, but they usually learn that you mean them no harm and stop the behavior with time. While the pecking may be off-putting to youngsters, it is a relatively harmless defense mechanism.

To lift a young chicken, grip it firmly but gently by the sides, to keep the young bird from flapping its wings. Very small chickens can be grasped by one hand, while older chicks may require the use of two hands. Allow the feet to slide between your fingers, or gently fold the legs into your hand.

2. Handling Adult Chickens

Even the quietest Chickens are averse to being lifted from the ground or held. Unfortunately, there are times when you will have to capture and hold your Chickens to inspect their health or move them.

Try to avoid stressing your birds unnecessarily when catching them. One of the best times to do so is during the night, when they will be slightly disoriented. If it is not possible to do so at night, consider herding the chickens into a room or building in which the lights can be turned off. Leave the lights off for about one hour before entering and trying to lift the animal.

If you are unable to catch your chicken (many Chickens are surprisingly agile and able to sneak away from you no matter how close you get) use the corralling technique to get the job done.

Corralling your chicken relies on gently herding it into an area where the walls function as a funnel. You can construct such a funnel with boards or any other barrier.

Once the chickens enter the wide end of the funnel, gently encourage them to travel to the narrow end. By doing so, the bird will become trapped, allowing you to get your hands on them.

Chickens are often lifted by the legs. Although the legs of chickens are strong enough to withstand this treatment, any rough movement while lifting a chicken by the legs may result in broken legs or feet.

Instead, to lift your chicken, grip it by the body. Approach the bird calmly to avoid startling it or encouraging it to flee. Grab the bird gently by the sides, keeping the wings folded flat against the birds' sides. Once you have the chicken lifted off the ground, place one of your hands under the bird and gently grasp the feet. This will reduce the chances of being scratched by the chicken's long toe nails.

Some prefer to let the chicken's feet protrude through the fingers, while others prefer to cup the feet in their hands, folding them up against the chicken's body. Either technique will work.

Once the chicken's feet are secure, press the chicken lightly against your body, allowing your arm to keep one wing pressed flat, while your body contains the other wing. This one-handed style allows your free hand to open and close doors, inspect injuries or any number of other tasks.

When releasing your chicken, place it down gently. Dropping your chicken roughly can cause them significant injury.

3. Talking to your chickens

Interacting with your pet chickens is actually very easy if you spend enough time with them. While holding and handling a chicken is essential to make your bird comfortable around you, you also need to in course talk to your chickens. This might sound a little unusual as the all the chickens do is cluck all day long. This is not true. Chickens have a language of their own that is actually quite simple to understand if you pay attention. Here are six simple tips that will help you talk to your pet chickens:

- **Listen closely and observe**

Just like other pets such as cats and dogs, chickens also have different tones and sounds that they use to communicate with one another. The best way to understand the different sounds produced is to watch your birds carefully. See what they are doing and listen to the noise that they are making. Slowly you will understand that the chicken makes a certain sound just before it wants to eat, the tone will change dramatically when it is about to enter a fight. The chicken will also change the way it clucks when it is in a heat etc. When you have mastered these variations you will be able to communicate with them better.

- **Learn from the mother**

Think of yourself as a baby chick that is still trying to learn the language of the birds. If you observe a hen interacting with her chicks you will also be able to pick up the language quite fast. For instance, if the mother hen is calling her chickens for feed the sound that she makes is very distinct and different. As you spend more time with the mother and her chick, you will be able to identify variations. Even the interactions between the rooster and the hens will teach you a lot about the language of the chickens

- **Create your own code words**

Like most pets, chickens can also be trained to respond to certain calls through conditioning. Create some words or phrases that you will repeat in a high pitch tone just before performing a certain task. For instance, you can shout out the words "Food is here" just before you fill the feeder to the chickens. The next time you say this phrase notice how the chickens come running to you. So it is possible to also use human words to talk to your chickens.

- **Understand the warning calls**

The most important purpose of talking to your chickens is to understand when they are in danger. Chickens make a very peculiar noise when they are in pain and when they have spotted a predator. Since this sound is not produced on a regular basis you must really listen intently to be able to identify it. Once you can associate a certain call with danger you will be able to protect your chickens better.

Once you have mastered the art of talking to your chickens you will be surprised at how wonderful they can be as your companions. Chickens can be really vocal and will narrate every painstaking detail of their life to you when you come home from a hard day's work. The best part is that they are great listeners too.

4. Herding Chickens

Once they are mature, the best approach to keeping Chickens is to avoid picking them up or otherwise handling them, unless absolutely necessary.

As with moving any animals, the easiest way to do so is to convince them to move themselves. This is not hard with chickens; they are seemingly always on the move. The problem arises when you need to get them to move where you want them to move. Essentially, you must learn to be a "chicken herder."

While they will never be accused of being as smart as dogs, dolphins or chimpanzees, chickens are surprisingly intelligent, and quick to learn routines. In fact, establishing routines is one of the best ways to make herding an easy task.

Ideally, when you open the bird's safe, secure sleeping quarters early in the morning, the chickens will walk outside and move in a more-or-less straight line to their daytime activity area. They should willingly march through the door and be on their way to eating, drinking, swimming and generally being a chicken. You can then – ideally – shut the gate behind them without ever having to put your hands on a chicken.

In the late afternoon, they should already be anticipating your arrival at the gate or door, and be ready to make the trek back to their sleeping quarters. Upon reaching the roost, a perfect flock makes its way inside and settles down for the night with very little encouragement necessary.

Chickens largely "go with the flow" so it is very helpful to herd flocks of some size. The chickens will take social cues from their neighbors, reinforcing their tendency to walk where you want them to go.

Begin teaching the chickens these behaviors from a very young age. If you begin training your chickens to move from place to place at a young age, they will be much easier to herd when they are larger. Additionally, by virtue of their small size, the young chicks are easier to control when this begins.

The easiest way to get your chickens accustomed to moving from one place to the other is to bribe them. For example, the chickens will usually be eager to exit their night roost once morning arrives. However, you will have to encourage them to go where you want them to go.

So, when you open the roost in the morning, move swiftly to the area you want the chickens to come to and lure them to follow with some of their favorite food. After doing this for a few days, they will begin to anticipate the routine and will naturally head to that area. Eventually, you can stop feeding them, once the behavior is the normal routine.

Stragglers who wander off or do not seem to be interested in the tasty treat require different strategies. Usually, chickens will flee when approached, so you can use this to your advantage.

While you are 20 yards (18 meters) or more away, begin circling behind the wandering chicken, so that the chicken is between you and where you want it to go. For example, if the chicken were at the center of a watch dial and you want it to go towards the 12 o'clock position, move so that you are standing at the 6 o'clock position.

Slowly start moving towards the chicken. Usually, the Chicken will begin to walk away from you, and towards the intended location. If other chickens are still heading in the same direction, it will help accelerate the process. The goal is not to stress, harass or frighten the bird.

If the chicken begins veering off course, adjust your position to keep it between you and the target area. Sometimes it can help to have a long stick or pole when doing so. With the long stick, tap the ground to get the chicken back on track.

For example, if the chicken begins moving off to the left, put the pole in your left hand. Using the increased reach offered by the stick, extend the tip of the stick past the chicken on the left, in order to encourage him to bring his course back to the right. Do not touch the bird with the stick, instead the goal is for the bird to see the stick and move the other way.

Some Chicken keepers employ dogs to herd their birds. This is a wonderful option if you have a dog who is suitable and trustworthy enough for the job. In addition to helping to herd the chickens, the dog will likely dissuade predators to some extent. Well-trained dogs that have bonded with the flock can provide effective security for the chickens.

5. Feather clipping

Clipping a chicken's flight feathers is a harmless and effective way of keeping the chickens from flying away. The only down side of clipping feathers, as opposed to pinioning, is that it must be performed every year. An additional benefit of clipping the birds' feathers is that you can perform this procedure yourself.

Clipping the wings of a chicken is a very simple procedure and is actually quite similar to clipping the nails of your pet cat or dog. It is only the vibrations that are experienced during the clipping that scares off the chicken. So, if they get a little edgy or restless, calm them down and continue with the clipping process. When you clip the feathers of your chicken be very careful, as there should be absolutely no traces of blood. Even if there is any bleeding it should be minimum. In case of any bleeding, you must ensure that you have a first aid kit around to control it.

It is best to clip the feathers of a chicken after the adult feathers have developed fully. If you feel like the flight of the bird is not really a problem, you can avoid clipping the feathers. The pin feathers that are present at the end of the body should never be tampered with. It is advisable to clip the feathers on both the sides of the body to help the bird remain balanced. Do not cut the feathers so short that your bird cannot fly at all. Instead, just cut it to a length that will not allow the bird to fly too high. Remember that flight is a defense mechanism. Stripping the bird of it entirely is not a god idea.

The idea is that if a fox, coyote or other land based predator threatens the chickens, they have a better chance of escaping if they have the ability to fly. Even though large roosters cannot get very far from the ground, intact wings will allow them to move and maneuver much more effectively than those who have had their wings altered.

Clipping feathers at home

Supplies that you need:

- Sharp scissors
- Rubber gloves
- An old towel
- A first aid kit

- A few treats to calm the bird down

The procedure

When you start to clip the feathers of your chicken, make sure that you have someone to assist you. You need someone who can hold the bird firmly while you clip the feathers.

- Decide who will hold the chicken. The person whom the chicken is most comfortable with must hold it.

- Gather the chicken. Even if it is a little stressed, you must keep your calm. Never chase the chicken around the place as it will stress the chicken out a lot. If you are not able to get hold of a particular chicken, leave it alone. You can get another bird from the flock in the meantime.

- To get a firm grip on the chicken, hold it by its legs. The body must be supported with your hand. Keep your hand open and flat and let the chicken rest there. Leave the wing that you want to clip free.

- When you are clipping the wings, talk to the bird in a tone that is soothing and comforting.

- Spread the wings fully. You should be able to see all the feathers properly.

- Now study the feathers. The first ten feathers that you can see from the outside of the wing are the flight feathers. You can identify them easily as they are longer than the other feathers. Sometimes, they are also of a different color. Just cut beyond the edge of the next layer. It is about 3 to 5 inches approximately.

- Use a swift cut to clip the wings. The scissors should be sharp. Even if they are slightly blunt, the bird will be hurt.

- Once the feathers have been clipped, give the bird a treat.

Have someone knowledgeable about birds demonstrate feather clipping the first time. In principle, the primary flight feathers are cut off with a pair of sharp scissors. Usually, the feathers on one wing are clipped, while the feathers on the other wing are left intact.

By removing just a few feathers, these large and heavy chickens become unable to achieve the necessary lift to fly.

If you do not wish to clip the bird's feathers yourself, most veterinarians and pet stores will provide the service for a small fee.

Some keepers elect to accept the possibility that their birds may fly away, as they do not appreciate the alternative. Another reason that some keepers opt for not pinioning or clipping their chicken's wings is that they do not want to "disarm" the birds. This is particularly common among keepers who allow their chickens to live in a free-range manner.

6. Hygiene is important

Like most other animals, chickens can carry germs that can make people sick. Some of these germs do not even make the chickens sick, but they can be very dangerous for people. It is always important to practice good hygiene to reduce the chances of contracting an illness.

Many chickens (and other birds) carry Salmonella bacteria in their digestive system. The bacteria are spread via the fecal-oral route, meaning that chickens pass the bacteria in their feces, where it can eventually make its way into the mouth of another chicken.

As the chickens excrete infective spores in their droppings, they find their way onto the chicken's feathers, feet and beaks, as well as throughout their habitats. The entire area should be considered to be covered in the bacteria.

If some of the bacteria gets on your skin, and then you inadvertently transfer some of it to your mouth, you can get sick. It only takes a few spores to cause the illness, so it can be quite easy to catch.

Accordingly, you must be sure to wash your hands after handling poultry or anything in their enclosure. Use an anti-bacterial soap and warm water. Be sure to scrub the tiny nooks and crannies of your hands, where bacteria are likely to persist. This includes your fingernails and the crevices in your knuckles.

It is a good idea to wash your clothing after interacting with the chickens as well. Some keepers keep a pair of slip-on boots handy for when they must enter the enclosure. This way, they do not have to wash their shoes repeatedly.

Salmonella is usually not very serious for healthy adults. However, young children, the elderly and those with compromised immune systems are extremely susceptible to the disease, and often develop serious complications. In rare cases, death can result.

The most common symptoms of the disease are gastrointestinal upset, abdominal cramps and a high fever. Most healthy adults recover from the disease without medical attention, but antibiotics and supportive care may be necessary for high-risk groups.

With this in mind, the Center for Disease Control and Prevention recommends that all live poultry be kept outdoors, and away from areas where people eat or drink. Furthermore, the CDC advises that children under 5 years of age be prevented from touching live poultry.

According to the CDC, live poultry are one of the most likely ways for people to contract the disease. Since the 1990s, more than 45 different outbreaks of the bacteria have originated from live poultry. These outbreaks have caused more than 220 hospitalizations and five deaths (Centers for Disease Control and Prevention, 2014).

Never, under any circumstances, should you use kitchen or bathroom sinks to wash tools or other accessories that have been in contact with the chickens.

Sometimes, a new bird may have infections that will prove fatal to chickens and other fowl present in your farm or garden. The only way to overcome this is by taking adequate measures to quarantine.

Quarantining requires you to keep the new bird away from the rest of the birds for at least 2 to 3 weeks. During this period, your new bird will require a separate coop or house to ensure that he does not mingle with the birds. Many chicken owners neglect quarantining to avoid the expense of an additional coop. However, it is worth the investment considering that the entire existing flock is in danger of infection.

Chapter 11: Transporting Your Chickens

If you are running a business with your chickens, you will have to occasionally transport your chickens. You may also have to take your chickens out to visit the vet or even take them out with you when you are travelling. So, it is important to know the safest means to get your chickens from one place to another.

1. Containers that you can use

When it comes to safe transportation, the first step is to find a container that your chicken can be comfortable in. There are two options that are best suited for chickens:

Plastic Tubs

Plastic transportation tubs are easy to make, and can often be created from recycled or repurposed materials, making them quite affordable. To transform a tub into a chicken-carrier, simply drill several 1-inch holes on the top and sides of the tub to provide ventilation. By placing the holes in this manner, air will be drawn in through the sides and vented out through the holes in the lid.

Place some dry straw at the bottom of the tub to provide comfort and to absorb liquids.

If not properly ventilated, this type of transportation vessel can become very damp and full of polluted air that can make your chicken very sick.

Opaque tubs are the best choice, as they will prevent the chickens from seeing the activity outside the container. This can stress them, making them more susceptible to illness. Transparent containers can be used, but they should be covered with a lightweight covering to prevent the chickens from becoming stressed.

Wire Cages

Wire cages are perhaps the most popular choice for transporting chickens. These are available commercially in a variety of styles, sizes and price points. The other primary benefits of wire cages are that they offer plenty of ventilation for the inhabitants, which can make them more comfortable in warm environments. However, the open nature of the cage means that these are messier than plastic tubs and odors, spilled water, food and feces are likely to escape the boundaries of the cage from time to time. In cold weather, such cages cannot be left exposed to the elements for extended periods of time.

2. Transportation choices

Once you have chosen the container that you want to keep your chickens in, you will have to choose the mode of transport. The mode of transport depends upon the distance that the chickens will be travelling. Remember that chickens find travelling rather stressful. So, if you plan to drive them for long distances, you must be prepared to have a really sick and upset bird in the back seat. Usually, there are three transportation options that are available to pet owners:

Your Personal Vehicle

If you have a car or a truck you can transport your chickens and chicks in them. When you re transporting chickens, you must remember that they are extremely fragile creatures. Chicks are, especially, prone to strangulation and broken bones when they are being transported.

It is a good idea to choose proper carriers to transport your chickens. Make sure that the size is just right to prevent them from falling and hurting themselves. The bedding should be soft and thick to provide ample cushioning. You must also ensure that food and water is available to the chickens. If you are transporting adult chickens, you might want to carry them in separate carriages. If you are transporting multiple birds, make sure that they are able to see their companions so that they feel secure. While transporting chicks, you must also provide them with a proper heat source to keep them warm.

Shipping

You may also use the postal services to transport your chickens. If you are considering shipping your chickens in overnight carriages, it is important for you to obtain a health certificate from a licensed veterinarian. This rule is applicable in most states. The certificate must be obtained at least 10 days prior to shipping

The best option is the bio- safe carrier that is used to transport birds. These carriers come with a lining that is water resistant. They also have air holes to ensure oxygen supply to the bird. A substance known as gro-gel plus may be used to keep your chickens hydrated during the flight. Ideally, you will require about 2 packets per chicken for an overnight flight. You can place the gel in plastic cups secured to the corners of the carriers so that the chickens have access to it throughout the journey.

It is advisable to take the package yourself to the airport that the chickens will fly out of. Your local post office will be able to give you that information. Make sure that the flight is non-stop. Chickens cannot make it more than one non-stop flight from one city to another. If you must make a stop, ensure that the second half of the journey is covered by road or rail.

Make sure that your carrier screams out that there are live birds in it. Although there are signs on the packages usually, you must ensure that you highlight this fact. This is because any live animal is treated differently from other cargo. They are transported in areas that are safe and comfortable.

It is a good idea to line the box with warm bedding. You must also make sure that the material you use gives the chicken proper foothold to prevent injuries due to skidding.

Shipping chickens in the beginning of the week is ideal as the staff remains the same. If you ship them anytime after Thursday, there is a higher possibility of mix ups. Shipping or air travel should be the last option when you are transporting your chickens. If you can avoid it, make sure you do to avoid unnecessarily traumatizing the birds.

Estimated Costs

The cost of shipping chickens, like any other shipment, depends entirely on the size of the package. Usually, a package containing less than 35 chicks is considered a small shipment. Additionally, if you are shipping them beyond zone 5, the costs will go up.

When you are shipping more than 35 chicks, the estimation of the cost is made per volume weight. This is because, the package is undoubtedly lighter. However, the space occupied by the package is large. This rule was introduced recently in 2007 as the boxes used to ship chickens took up quite a large amount of space. So, even if you are shipping a box that only weighs 10 pounds, the post office will equate it to 17 pounds.

If you are sending the shipment to zone 5 or beyond, it is recommended that you transport at least 60 chicks per box as the cost will not change with weight.

Another added expense is when you request for express mail. There is a $10-$15 (£6- 10) additional charge with express mail. Usually birds are sent via Priority mail. The truth is that the time taken by priority mail and express mail is almost the same. There is no real difference.

All in all, you will spend about $50/ £30 for the shipping itself. In addition to that you will pay $50/ £30 for the box and the supplies necessary to ensure a safe trip for your birds.

3. Safety Regulations

Regardless of the type of transportation vessel you use, always be sure that the container is securely strapped into your vehicle, by using seatbelts, bungee cords or straps. In addition to keeping your chickens safer in the event of an accident, it will help prevent the container from sliding around – something that can cause you to have an accident in the first place!

Never leave chickens unattended in a hot car. The glass windows create a greenhouse effect, which can cause the internal temperature to rise to dangerous levels very quickly. Chickens can and have died from being left in a hot car.

Avoid playing loud music or driving erratically while chauffeuring your chickens. Ultimately, a car ride can be a very stressful experience for your feathered friends, and you should try to keep the event as stress-free as possible.

Chapter 12: Managing The Eggs

Buff Orpingtons are prolific egg layers, laying close to 200 eggs each year. They often do not restrict the egg-laying to a nest. So, if you are interested in the egg business, you must be alert to collect the eggs as and when they are laid. This prevents breakage and wastage of the egg.

1. Collecting Eggs

Usually chickens tend to lay eggs early in the morning or late at night. When you are collecting eggs and your chicken is still laying eggs, it is best that you allow the chicken to roost for at least two hours before you proceed to select the next batch of eggs. Eggs must always be collected in the plastic egg trays. It is advisable to keep the dirty and clean eggs separate.

If you are selecting eggs for incubation, you must make sure that the egg is not underweight, cracked or molted and poor in texture. These eggs are less likely to hatch and are better for human consumption.

2. Cleaning

Eggs must be cleaned as soon as they have been collected to ensure that they do not get spoiled. There are several microorganisms that might make their way in to the shell if the eggs are not cleaned. To remove the mud and manure, the eggs can be rubbed gently with steel wool. Wiping them after this is also an option.

You must never wash the eggs as the contents will shrivel up, reducing hatchability. Instead, you can choose fumigation to clean the eggs thoroughly.

3. Storage

If you do not have enough eggs to incubate, you may have to store the ones that you already have. These eggs can be stored for a maximum of seven days before they are incubated. It is best to store them in cold conditions. Maintain the temperature at about 13 degrees Celsius, with 75% relative humidity. Always keep the pointed end of the egg down for maximum hatchability.

4. Hatching the eggs

Buff Orpington Chickens are prolific egg layers. If you decide to have your own flock from these eggs you need to hatch the eggs. You can either hatch the eggs naturally in hatcheries or can choose some artificial methods. Either way you need to have fertilized eggs. You will need a broody hen to sit on them if you choose to hatch the eggs naturally. A broody hen normally sits in her nesting box and will not budge. The brooding time may vary. Some of them may brood for longer period. This could happen even if the eggs are not collected on daily basis. The time taken for eggs to hatch is normally three to four weeks and that would be the brooding time.

If you choose to hatch the eggs artificially here are a few methods you can follow:

Hatching by using incubators

Incubators can be bought from farm supply stores. These incubators should be placed on a plain surface inside the home. The incubator must be kept away from sunlight as per the instructions mentioned with the equipment since it can affect the temperature inside. The above steps when followed provide a secure environment for hatching the eggs.

Incubators are of two types: Forced air incubator and still air incubator. In the forced air incubator the heat is uniformly spread where as in the still air incubator there is no movement of heat. The temperature in the forced air incubator should be maintained at 100 degrees Fahrenheit and at 102 degrees Fahrenheit in the still-air incubator.

You could make your own incubator if you have a proper plan, the required equipment and skill.

Turning of the Eggs

The eggs need to be turned regularly. It can either be turned automatically with egg turners or could be done manually. If the eggs are turned manually then one side of the egg should be marked with an X and the other side should be marked with an O. The egg should be given a half turn that is, it should be turned 180 degrees. Eggs normally are turned 5 times in a day. The whole process should be done very gently as if you were the parent of the egg.

The eggs should be turned each day till day 18. The number of times the eggs are rotated in a day should be in odd numbers. If this is done then the same side of the embryo will be rotated. After the 18th day the chick is ready to hatch and it should be kept still. Around the 21st day the hatching of the chick will begin and all the eggs would be hatched within 24 hours.

Eggs that are received from other places or imported need a long time to hatch since they have to get used to the new environment. Normally the hatcheries take utmost care to deliver the eggs safely but at times they tend to get twisted and they have to be set to be straight. The eggs should be placed with the larger side facing up in a tidy egg carton which will stabilize the air bubbles and return to their place. The eggs should be left to stabilize with the larger side facing up for a minimum of 12 hours. Avoid washing the eggs since it would wash away the protective layer making it susceptible to disease and infection.

Settings of the incubator

The incubator settings have to be done 24 hours prior to receiving the chicks. Temperatures should be between 99 degrees to 100 degrees Fahrenheit and humidity levels also to be adjusted properly. The temperature in the incubator will decrease the first time the eggs are put inside the incubator. This is because on opening the incubator a portion of the warm air would be let out and the temperature of transported eggs are cooler. Before the eggs are put in the incubator the temperature should be constant and stable and it would take at least 4 hours for the temperature to stabilize. Every setting should be appropriate before placing the eggs in the incubator since any minor adjustment could destroy the embryos. Humidity levels should be 58% to 60% from day 1 to day 18 in the incubator. Thereafter it could be increased gradually to 65%. The eggs need more humidity as they age in order to make it easier for the birds to adjust to the surrounding.

Normally the incubators are designed with a water pan. If you are making your own incubator place a sponge soaked in water in the incubator along with the eggs. A slight variation in humidity is allowed since it is not possible to get the ideal humidity levels. Humidity levels should be closely monitored. Low humidity will result in the shells sticking to the chick or may result in producing either small chicks or the navel of the chick would be rough. High humidity will result in a yolk sac which is unabsorbed and this will spread on the baby bird.

High-tech incubators are automatic and all the settings are automatically done. So it is much easier with High tech incubators. If a basic incubator, for instance, the one made of Styrofoam is being used then it needs close monitoring though it works well. Temperatures can be checked using Probe Thermometers.

The most important aspect of the incubator is ventilation. Ensure proper circulation of air in the incubator. Poor circulation of air would result in retention of gases which could prove toxic to eggs. Vents can be placed either on the top, bottom or on the side of the incubator. During incubation these vents should be slowly opened so that when the eggs are ready to hatch the vents are fully opened. Maintaining proper humidity levels is very critical. Humidity levels should be from 58% to 60% from the 1st day to the 18th day and raised to 65% after that. Maintaining proper humidity levels result in formation of healthy well- formed chicks.

There could be a bad smell emanating from the incubator if there are one or more bad eggs in the incubator. At that time you should remove the bad eggs from the incubator. If the bad eggs are not removed it may explode due to the built up gases in the incubator and may spoil the other eggs too. If the eggs take longer than 25 days to hatch then it can be presumed that will not hatch at all these eggs can be discarded.

The incubator should be opened only to add water after the 18th day. After 18th day the vents should be closed. The chicks will be provided with stable environment by keeping the vents closed. New born chicks will be delicate and their immune system will be weak at this stage and so should not be touched often. After a few weeks these chicks will be moving around and will be ready to play with.

Candling is a fun process for adults and children which is used to check the actual development of the chicks. For this process you should turn the lights off and an egg should be removed from the incubator. You can see a shadow within if you hold a flashlight, slide projector or a candle behind the egg. The eggs should be placed back in the incubator in 20 to 30 minutes. The broader end of the egg will have the embryo with the blood vessels around it. Candling can be done at any stage of development but the chicks are more recognizable eighth day onwards. Possibly, a beating heart or a vein or an active chicken will be visible. There will be a black spot on a fertile egg which will develop to become a chick. If the egg is clear then it is an unfertilized egg. The yolk will be surrounded by a blood ring or a dark spot if the embryo is dead.

To make your own candling system you need the following materials:

- Sealed-beam floodlight bulb of 60-watt
- Light base of Ceramic
- Cord of Old Lamp

- Utility box measuring 4 inch by 4 inch
- Connector with clamp for non-metallic cable
- Scrap wood piece for mounting base
- Cardboard box with a small hole
- A roll of black electric tape

Directions to make the candling system:

- Make a hole at the side of Cardboard box and fix the clamp connector on the outside.
- Pass the lamp cord with $3/4^{th}$ inch bare ends through the connector and leave 6" of the cord inside the box
- 4" x 4" box to be screwed down to the piece of wood being used as the base and the connector screws should be tightened.
- Lamp cord should be attached to the light base. A wire should go on each screw no matter which wire to which screw
- Lamp base should be attached with the screws that came with it.

The light bulb should now be placed in. Cut a small hole in the cardboard box and commence the candling. Drill a hole big enough to see the egg. The candler should not be left unattended since the heated bulb can cause fire.

Preventing the Egg Eating habit

Once the hens get the taste of broken egg then they tend to make it a habit over a period of time. To avoid this habit it is important to manage a way so that the hen never has a chance to taste a broken egg.

The following are the Prevention Management practices:

1. Less Traffic in the Nesting Area. Congested nesting area is one of the reasons for egg breakage. Hens start eating eggs when there are broken eggs. The following precautions can be taken to avoid egg breakage.

a)   4 to 5 hens in a flock should have 12 x 12" nest. There should be a minimum of 6 nesting boxes. These should be placed at a distance of 4 feet from each other and at least 2 feet above the ground.

b)   Lack of protective padding causes cracking of eggs. Nests should always contain 2 inches of clean nesting material.

c)   Brooding hens occupy most of the nesting space. So they should be removed from the nesting area.

2. **Nutrition.** Oyster shells are a major source of calcium supplement that keeps the shell strong. The hens should be fed with Oyster shells along with a generous amount of other feed.

Eggs shells should be fed to the hens only after smashing them. If the hens get a taste of the shell with the egg and if they can associate the egg to the shell then they will get into the habit of picking the fresh eggs in the coop.

3. Minimizing Stress

a) Hens get nervous and will develop picking habits when the lights are bright. So avoid bright lights in the Coops.

b) Hens should not be scared out of the nesting boxes. Eggs in the nesting box break with the sudden movement and the hens will get a taste of egg and will develop the habit of egg eating.

4. Egg Eating Outsider. The Eggs can be eaten by outside predators, for instance, snakes, weasels etc. The beak and sides of the heads of hens eating eggs will have dried yolk. Also the hens eating eggs will be wandering around the nest looking for fresh laid eggs.

An egg eating hen should immediately be removed from the flock once spotted. The eating habit will multiply if allowed to continue. Once a hen is allowed to eat eggs the others will follow.

Prevention is the only way to stop the egg eating habit. Hens normally lay eggs before 10.00 a.m. Eggs should be collected frequently and early in the morning. If the eggs are allowed to stay longer in the Coop they may either break or be eaten.

5. On Hatching

After hatching, the chicks can be kept in the incubator for 4 to 5 hours. They need this time in the incubator to stay warm and to dry out. Chicks get all their nutrition from their shell for almost 48 hours after hatching and so they can survive without food or water for 48 hours. After 48 hours some food such as chick feed and water can be put in the starter box so that they get used to it. If the chicks are allowed to feed after 48 hours they will not be stressed. Initially they should be picked up and taken to the feeder. Some chicks that are adventurous can get their food but the timid ones end up without food since they are overpowered and pushed out. So you need to keep watch and ensure that your brood is getting the required nourishment.

The chicks are too delicate and immature in the absence of a mother hen. At this stage it is advisable to keep the chicks in the starter box soon after hatching. Your starter box can be a large box made of cardboard with a heat lamp inside. The box should measure 2 feet by 2 feet and 1 foot high covered with a mesh. The box of this size can accommodate about ten newly hatched chicks. But as they grow they occupy more space. The temperature in the box also should be regulated. During the first week the temperature should be maintained at 90 to 95 degrees Fahrenheit and should be gradually reduced by 5 degrees every week till the room temperature is attained. To monitor the temperature a thermometer can be used. If the temperature is very high the chicks will chirp loudly and will stand apart opening their mouths wide. If it is too cold then they chirp in a shrill tone. If they are chirping in a soft tone then the temperature is just right. Controlled temperature will keep the chicks healthy and comfortable.

The starter box should have at least 2 inches of bedding. The bedding should either be made of wood chips or a removable mesh wire. Wood chips are a better option since they are suitable for the chicks' tender toes. Avoid using newspaper or slick bedding as they are not suitable for the growth of the chicks' feet and legs. Wood chips are a good option but you should keep a close watch since some chicks feed on the shavings which may choke them. Keep a close watch and ensure that the chicks do not feed on things that are not good for them, are not being smothered by other chicks.

Chicks are very fond of water. So make plenty of water available. When you feed the chick with water for the first time, dip only the beak in the water ensuring that the feathers do not get wet. Chicks are very susceptible to chill and so keeping them dry is mandatory. To sanitize the water feeders and waterers wash them daily with a mild detergent.

Chicks poop very frequently so make sure to keep their box and bedding tidy to avoid growth of bacteria. Check the behind of the chicks regularly. Feces sticking to the backside of the chick block the flow of poop and so should be washed with a warm damp cloth and toothpick. This cleaning should necessarily be done since the blockage of the poop can be fatal. If the blockage keeps continuing and you cannot handle it then take the bird to a vet. The area around the toes also should be cleaned since manure stick around the toes. If not cleaned, other birds may peck at the toes. Pecking can cause the chick to walk on the side of its feet causing crookedness.

6. Taking Your Chickens Outdoors

You can take your chicks outside when they are 4 to 5 weeks old under supervision. If they have to go unsupervised they should be at least 8 weeks old. Your chicks can be introduced to your adult flock when they are 8 weeks old. Some breeds like Leghorn mature faster than the others and so their timeline requires to be adjusted. Before you take them outdoors they should be fully feathered and should be able to take care of themselves. The weather conditions and the surroundings they will be in when they are outside also need to be considered. Roosters and some of the breeds like the Faverollos are very active and you need to take them outdoors earlier as they do not like to stay confined for a longer time.

Chickens love to stroll in gardens foraging for worms and bugs on grass. They need to dig and scratch with their claws. Dirt is also necessary for the Chickens. They roll on the dust instead of bathing with water which enables them to dry the oil coating on their feathers. In order to rid themselves of built up oil Chickens preen themselves. They also love to sunbathe which provides them with Vitamin D. Sunbathing helps them to maintain overall health.

7. Handling Sick Chicks

You need to keep a close watch on the Chicks for any changes. If you observe that some chicks are looking weaker or having problems with their health after weeks then you should react immediately. If you are raising show birds then they should meet all the specified standards for the exhibitions. If the chicks are weak and look unhealthy and are not perfect they will be disqualified. So if you notice any sick or deformed birds then immediately separate them from the rest of the show birds. If deformed or weak birds are bred there are chances that the same gene will be reproduced which will be of no use to you. Also even if you are raising the chicks for meat or to have them as pets they need to be healthy and well formed.

Chickens are normally affected by fowl pox or New Castle disease. If you notice that your chicks have some form of canker sores then they are affected by fowl pox and if you notice respiratory disorders in your chicks then they are affected by New Castle disease. To prevent your chicks from these diseases vaccinating them should be a mandatory part of your raising program. The right time to inoculate your chicks is after they are

8 weeks old. Ensure that all the birds are vaccinated. Even a single affected bird can spread the disease to your entire brood very rapidly.

If your chicks have to be medicated with pills then you can give the whole pill if they can gobble the pill by pecking at it. Otherwise pound the pill and mix it with the treat meant for the chickens. You can either crush the pill with a spoon or a plate by pressing them hard on the pill. You can also mix the powder with water and pour it down the bird's mouth using an eyedropper. If the entire flock has to be medicated then the pills should be crushed using a coffee grinder or a small mixer. Then the powder should be mixed with water and should be fed to the chickens individually. You will observe that the chickens normally eat throughout the day. They will be nibbling with something or the other throughout the day. But early mornings and late night are the times when they are the hungriest. This is the right time to medicate your chickens so that they consume the entire treat that is mixed with the medication.

8. Managing Chicken Stress

Chickens are very sensitive beings and can be disturbed with the slightest variations in their surroundings. They are very sensitive to noise and climate changes. They get stressed when the surrounding is overcrowded and noisy. They also get stressed if they come into contact with other animals or if they are separated from the flock they are familiar with. Stress in the chickens will lower their PH level which will weaken their immune systems and will make them more susceptible to diseases. Always take care to speak softly when you are approaching the bird. Keep your tone very soft and soothing. Keep them away from loud children, bright light and other animals.

Here are a few tips to prevent stress in your chickens:

• The coop should be adequately lit and secure
• Their home should be tidy.

- Enough space should be provided
- Their coop should be kept warn in winter and cool in summer
- Familiarize them with people by interacting with the flock regularly
- Children should be taught to respect the birds

Chapter 13: Health And Well Being

The health of your Buff Orpington Chicken is your responsibility. If you are unable to take good care of your birds, they may become infected or may even die. The most difficult thing with diseases related to chickens is that they spread to the entire flock even before you can notice it. So, you must be vigilant and watch out for some obvious signs that will tell you that your bird is unwell.

The good thing about chickens is that they have very unique characteristics and behavior patterns. Any deviation from normalcy is a sign that your chicken is either unwell, or is stressed for various reasons. There are some common symptoms that you must look out for if you suspect that your chicken has fallen sick:

- Reduced levels of activity
- Not socializing. A sick chicken will keep to itself and will occupy a lonely corner in the pen
- Loss of appetite
- The volume of activity is reduced
- Sudden deviation from normal activity
- Sticky poop that is found on the vent of the coop
- Eyes that are dull or half closed
- Change in the color of the poop or diarrhea
- Sleeping for long hours
- Constant Sneezing
- Puffed up feathers
- Feathers that are ragged and not preened properly.
- Sudden Weight Loss
- Swelling in the joints
- Breathing with the mouth open

Chickens are fabulous creatures in several ways. One very interesting display of group behavior is assisting other birds when they are unwell or injured. You can tell that a chicken is unwell even by observing the behavior of other chickens around him.

For instance, if your chicken has a broken wing, you will see that other chickens will gently hold up the upper feathers to provide assistance. They will also nudge and flock around unwell chickens in a caring and affectionate manner. However, you must be aware of one important thing. The above mentioned signs can be observed only if you are very vigilant. Usually, chickens are great at hiding their illnesses. Therefore, many owners are unable to tell if their pet chickens are unwell until it is too late. So, never neglect even the slightest deviation in your bird's behavior.

1. Bacterial, Viral and Fungal Infections

New Castle's Disease

This is a highly contagious disease that is very common in chickens. The disease can have three intensities: Mildly pathogenic, moderately pathogenic and highly pathogenic.

Symptoms
- Hoarse chirps in young chicks
- Watery discharge from the nostrils
- Gasping
- Swelling of the face
- Trembling
- Twisted neck
- Reduced appetite and thirst

Causes

- The Newcastle virus
- Transmitted through feed deliverers, dirty equipment and even contaminated shoes
- Passed to the egg
- Airborne
- From other birds

Treatment

- No specific treatment
- Antibiotics can be provided for 3 to 5 days
- Reducing brooding temperature

Prevention

- Vaccination
- Good Sanitation

Botulism

Symptoms

- Limber neck with reduced muscular control
- Loss of Muscular control in limbs and wings
- Difficulty in swallowing properly

Causes

- Infection due to toxins produced by Clostridia bacterium

Treatment

- Chickens should be kept away from stagnant pools and dirty areas
- Provide fresh drinking water
- Epsom Salt may be added to the drinking water of the chickens

Coccidiosis

Symptoms

- Blood in the droppings
- Weight loss

- Persistent illness

Causes

- Contact with droppings of birds containing coccicdia. These are protozoa, making it difficult to eliminate them with just antibiotics.

Treatment

- Adding anticoccidial medication to the drinking water
- Keep the ground clean
- Feed them regularly

Chicken Virus enteritis

Entritis is very rare in chickens. However, if a bird is affected by it, it is going to die in all probability. The infection might be viral or sometimes, bacterial. This condition is usually contagious and is acquired when domestic chickens come in contact with wild birds.

Symptoms

- Listlessness in birds
- Reddish or pinkish droppings

Treatment

- Antibiotic powders that dissolve in water. You must only give medicated water to the infected birds.

Chicken Hepatitis

Hepatitis is most often contracted by chicks and is fatal once the bird has been infected. This condition normally occurs when the chicken is less than six weeks old.

Symptoms

- Severe spasticity
- Displacement of eyeballs within the orbit
- Paralysis
- Sudden death

Causes

- Hepatitis is caused due to two viruses in chickens- Chicken Hepatitis Virus-1 and Chicken Hepatitis Virus-2. Infection by DHV-1 is more severe, leading to the death of the chicken within two hours of the appearance of clinical symptoms.

Treatment

Chicken Hepatitis can only be prevented with vaccination.

Riemerellaanatipestifer infection

This infection is fatal in chickens. It is also found in other breeds of poultry like turkeys and geese. This condition normally occurs when the chicks are between 1-8 weeks old.

Symptoms

- Stunted Growth
- Coughing
- Anorexia
- Diarrhea
- Convulsions
- Localized infections in chronic cases

Cause

Infection by gram-negative bacteria that belongs to *Flavobacteriacae* family.

Treatment

- Good Husbandry
- Antibiotics
- Vaccination

Fowl Cholera

Fowl cholera is a bacterial infection that can infect Chickens. Caused by the bacteria Pasteurella multocida, the disease is highly contagious, and found in waterfowl populations worldwide.

Unfortunately, the symptoms of fowl cholera vary widely. In many cases, one of the first clues is the sudden die off of a large number of birds that were formerly without symptoms. When symptoms are present, they often include intestinal disturbance, rapid breathing, anorexia and depression.

Cholera is usually transmitted via water sources, such as wetlands and ponds. Fowl cholera is a zoonotic, so it is important to recognize the symptoms of the disease and seek treatment for the birds, as it can be transmitted to humans.

Antibiotics are usually prescribed to treat infected birds, but they do not always work. In a 1992 study, fowl cholera was fatal to approximately 50 percent of the birds in the study. The other half of the birds recovered after treatment with antibiotics (Nakamine M, 1992). However, many birds die after treatment stops, which shows that the disease has not been eliminated, but only suppressed.

When a flock is infected with Fowl Cholera, the area must be completely depopulated and cleaned thoroughly to prevent further infection.

Chicken Parvovirus

Chicken parvovirus is a disease that is especially dangerous to Chickens. Primarily a disease of young Chickens, the virus does not cause symptoms in chickens older than five weeks of age.

When young chickens become infected with this deadly pathogen, they only have an approximately 20 percent chance of survival. Hatchlings and young chicks transmit the virus between themselves, but chickens can also catch the virus from their mother.

Sick chicks exhibit signs of nervousness, huddle together in a tight cluster and may drag their feet behind themselves. Digestive disturbances may also occur, although the birds do not lose feathers as geese do when infected with the goose parvovirus.

There is no treatment for the pathogen except establishing very strict quarantines and implementing a vaccination program. Day-old chicks can be vaccinated, but the adults must be given boosters regularly to prevent passing the virus to the young, and susceptible, chicks.

Avian Influenza

Chickens can contract avian influenza, and there is a possibility that they can transmit this illness to humans. Since 1997, the Centers for Disease Control and Prevention states that humans have contracted several different strains of the disease.

While wild birds seldom die from the disease, avian influenza is often fatal to captive birds, who often develop more virulent strains of the virus. Waterfowl seem to be especially susceptible to the disease.

A 2001 report documented that the disease caused nervousness and death in a backyard flock of Chickens and domestic geese (Anser anser domestica). Upon further examination, the chickens were found to have incurred damage to their nervous systems and pancreases (Mutinelli, 2001).

Respiratory Problems in Chickens

If you observe your chicken breathing with the mouth open, there are chances that he is suffering from respiratory ailments. Other common signs of respiratory problems are sounds like wheezing or whistling when the chicken is breathing.

It is important to take care of respiratory problems at the earliest as they might be fatal to the chicken. Chickens are also unable to function properly and carry out regular activities like foraging and running if they are unable to breathe properly. When chickens become inactive, they also become severely stressed, leading to secondary problems like behavior changes.

One important thing that you must remember when you notice that your chicken has respiratory problems is that you must consult your vet before taking any action. This is because problems related to the lungs of birds can be quite complex. Remember that the lungs of birds are modified or adapted to aid flying. As a result, the treatment of respiratory problems should be left to the specialists.

Chronic Respiratory Problems

One chronic respiratory problem that is common to chickens is called Alpergliosis. It is also known as brooder pneumonia or mycotic pneumonia. The symptoms of this disease are as follows:

- Labored breathing
- Hunching of the spine to aid breathing
- Whistling or wheezing noises while breathing.

Causes

Apergillosis is usually predominant in birds during the monsoon season. This is because the bedding might develop molds due to the moisture. Sometimes, poor sanitary conditions may also lead to aspergillosis.

Treatment

- Use of fungicides
- Better management of the pen
- Storage of food in dry and cool conditions
- Use of bedding material that is resistant to molds.

2. Digestive Problems

Most of the digestive problems in birds are related to their crop. The crop is that part of the chicken where the food goes immediately after feeding. You will notice a slight bulge in this region when your chicken has just eaten. If the bulge does not disappear overnight, it is a problem. There are two conditions that you must look out for in Chickens.

Sour Crop

Symptoms

- Swollen Mucus Membranes
- Appearance of an apple lodged in the neck
- Lesions around the neck and mouth

Causes

Sour Crop is usually caused by yeast infections in the crop of the bird. This condition is dangerous as it may damage the esophagus or even strangulate the bird, leading to death.

Treatment

- Withhold food for one day
- Provide clean and fresh drinking water only
- Massage the crop
- Drop olive oil into the crop to help it reduce in size

Sour Crop must not persist for more than 3 days. If it does, it is recommended that you consult your vet.

Blocked Crop

This condition is also known as impacted crop. As the name suggests, this condition occurs when the crop of the chicken gets blocked.

Symptoms

- Difficulty in swallowing
- Crop that is hard to touch
- Reduced Appetite
- Foul Smell from the Beak

Causes
- Consumption of foods that are too fibrous or tough
- Consumption of long strands of straw
- Lack of water

Treatment

- Provide your chicken with ample drinking water.
- If the condition persists, your vet may surgically remove the blockage in the crop.

3. Reproductive Diseases

Egg Binding

Egg binding can occur for a number of reasons. The formed egg may be too large to pass through the shell gland or the vagina, the chicken may have hypocalcaemia (calcium deficiency) or it may have sustained injury to its vent or vagina.

This often occurs in birds that are of advanced age, extremely young age or are overweight. While the retained egg obstructs the passageway, the chicken's body continues producing eggs behind it. Ultimately, this can lead to ruptures or eggs being deposited into the abdominal cavity.

Regardless of the reason it occurs, egg binding is a medical emergency. Chickens that are having difficulty expelling an egg may appear nervous, agitated or depressed. They may walk or pace excessively, as well as exhibit strange body postures.

Unfortunately, this condition is most often noted upon necropsy, as the birds often die before their owner has noticed the symptoms.

If you suspect that a female is egg bound, contact your veterinarian immediately.

Oviduct Prolapse

Sometimes, the oviduct protrudes in the lower region. This condition usually occurs when the chicken has difficulty in passing the egg out.

Treatment

- Provide calcium and phosphorous supplements
- Feed should only include layers pellets
- Keep the chicken warm
- Oral medication or injections if the problem persists.

Meritis

Bacterial infection of the oviduct, leading to inflammation is known as meritis.

Symptoms

- Persistent vaginal discharge
- Loss of appetite
- Lethargy

Treatment

- Antibodies administered orally or through injections

Peritonitis

Peritonitis is usually the result of an ovarian prolapse. When the egg fails to make its way into the oviduct but goes into the abdominal cavity instead, peritonitis occurs. The lining of the abdomen called the peritoneum gets infected.

Symptoms

• Swelling around the abdomen
• Diarrhea
• Sudden Death

Treatment

• Antibiotics have been effective in some cases.

4. Other Problems

Frostbite

While Chickens often tolerate cold temperatures well, one of the first problems they are likely to experience in very cold temperatures is frostbite. Frostbite is easier to prevent than to treat, so always be sure that your chickens have a shelter that allows them to escape inclement weather. In extreme cases, frostbite can be fatal.

One of the reasons that Chickens are so susceptible to frostbite is that they are warm-climate chickens, who dip their heads frequently in the water. When they pull their heads back out, their delicate facial tissue is wet and exposed to the cold and wind. Their feet sustain damage when the chickens walk on cold, wet ground or snow for extended lengths of time.

If you see that your chickens feet, face or bill have areas that are black, cracked or ulcerated, visit your veterinarian for treatment and fortify their shelter to provide more warmth.

Abraded Feet

Although they look sturdy, the feet of Chickens are very sensitive to rough surfaces. In severe cases, the chickens can develop serious, systemic infections if the wounds are not cleaned and treated properly.

If you notice wounds or abrasions on your chickens' feet, take them to the veterinarian for treatment. Your veterinarian will likely clean the wound, apply some antibiotics and schedule a follow up exam.

After visiting your veterinarian, it is crucial to fix the problem to prevent further injury. Ensure that all surfaces that the chickens must walk on are smooth and clean to reduce the likelihood of complications.

It also may be necessary to keep your chicken in an enclosed space while he heals. The bacteria on the ground and in the water may cause the wounds to become infected.

Missing Feathers or Wounds

Chickens lose feathers for a variety of reasons, including infighting, poor nutrition and sickness. Additionally, chickens molt periodically to replace their feathers.

While the first molt you witness may cause you to be concerned, you will soon learn the cycle of molting and what it looks like when the birds go through the process.

However, it is important to distinguish normal molting (and incidental feather loss that happens from normal activity from time to time) from that associated with infighting or disease.

Visit your veterinarian if you cannot determine the cause of the lost feathers. Your veterinarian can perform tests to determine whether or not your chicken is suffering from an illness. Missing feathers will usually re grow with the next molting cycle.

Tangled String and Similar Wounds

Chickens can become entangled in a number of man-made substances, including string, fishing line, rope, netting, plastic or wire. In some circumstances – such as when chickens become tangled while in the water – this can be a deadly problem. Because these types of problems often cause chickens to flail about and struggle frantically to escape, be alert for panicked, struggling chickens. However, if the chicken is able to move about relatively normally, they may not exhibit high stress levels, and just try to make the best of the situation.

If you find that your chicken is tangled, try to keep it calm while you work to remove the foreign material. Grasp the chicken gently but firmly with your arm, while you work the string or wire off with the other hand. It often helps to have another person assist with the procedure.

If your chicken is stressed or upset by the activity, it sometimes helps to cover his/her head with a soft, dark cotton bag or towel. Do not wrap it tightly around its head, but let it drape freely. Alternatively, you can take the chicken to a dark area, which may also help to calm it down.

After removing all of the material, inspect the chicken for wounds. Often, while attempting to free themselves, chickens cause fishing lines or similar materials to cut into their skin. If any significant cuts are apparent, consider seeking veterinary attention, as infection is a strong possibility.

If the wounds are minor, use a wound wash or clean water to cleanse the area. Keep the chicken in a clean, dry, warm environment for a few days to ensure he/she heals without developing an infection.

Fixing a Broken Wing

The wings of chickens form and important part of their defense mechanism and also help them maintain the balance of their bodies when they are running or walking upright. So, a broken wing is a serious issue that must be taken care of immediately.

Of course, you will require the assistance of a waterfowl vet to help take care of the issue completely. However, first aid is necessary when you have a chicken with a broken wing to ensure that the condition does not become worse.

There are several reasons why a chicken might have a broken wing. If the drakes become aggressive, they are capable of getting injured in fights. Mating among chickens is so aggressive that, many times, the female might be attacked by several males at one time and actually breaks her wings. In addition to this, an attack by a predator may also cause serious injuries to chickens. There are always chances of the wing getting stuck in wires or mesh, leading to injuries like broken bones. Whatever the cause, broken wings can be very painful and must be taken care of at the earliest.

A broken wing can cause excruciating pain and can lead to a lot of stress if left unattended. Sometimes, broken wings may also be accompanied by serious cuts and wounds that need to be treated properly to avoid infections. So it is necessary for you to be able to identify a broken wing.

When a wing is broken, it will hang very low. You will notice that it is displaced and is much lower than the other wing.

The first step to treating a broken wing is to gain the confidence of the bird to be able to handle it. Usually when they are injured, birds tend to become more defensive. Especially after an attack, a chicken will not really be very easy to hold and take into your care.

First, give the chicken some feed and also some water. If he actually begins to eat, it is much easier for you to get a grip on it. However, after a traumatizing injury, your chicken is less likely to want to eat. In such cases, the only option you have is to chase the chicken to a corner and then catch it. You must be firm in your grip and must gently hold the wings down, taking great care with the broken wing. The best way to calm a chicken down is to set her in an isolated spot or even a small cage which is well lit and warm.

You must approach an injured chicken only when you are certain that it has calmed down completely. Failing this, you will find yourself going through the entire process of calming it down again.

Gently examine the bird for wounds and cuts that might be bleeding. These wounds must be washed to remove any impurity that might lead to infection. The wound can be washed with some lukewarm water or even iodine solution. If you have an antiseptic that you have used before, you may apply it.

The next step is to provide a splint or support of the broken wing. You can use sticky gauze or even veterinary tape for this purpose. Hold the wing in the natural position first. It must be held against the body of the bird to make sure that it heals in its natural position. Once the wing is in place, it needs to be bound to the body securely. Take the gauze or the tape around the body of the bird. The objective of the gauze and the tape is to ensure that the wing is immobilized. However, if you tie it too tightly, it might affect the breathing of the bird.

When you wrap the gauze, take it over the broken wing, around the body and under the wing that is functional. This will not restrict the movement of the other wing.

Usually, broken wings take about 4 weeks to heal completely. It is best that you keep the chicken in a cage and in isolation until the wing is completely healed. The quality of food must be very good during the healing period. Plenty of water must also be available for the bird to drink. In this period, if the gauze or tape becomes soiled, you may change it.

While you are changing the gauze, if you notice that the chicken is able to move the wing comfortably, you can remove the dressing. If not, you can take the gauze off after four weeks. Now your bird is also ready to mingle with the rest of the flock and carry on with his routine.

If your bird has been attacked by a predator, he might require vaccinations or shots to ensure that there is no infection. Even in case of open wounds, it is best recommended that you have it checked by a waterfowl professional.

Beak Problems

The beak of chickens is not a mere defense organ, it is very important in indicating the health of the bird. Any abnormality or deformation in the bill indicates that the bird may have several underlying health issues that require immediate attention.

Signs

There are some common and obvious problems that owners might notice with the bills of their pets:

- Rotting or discolored beaks
- Cracks in the beak
- Dry beaks that are peeling
- Bruised beaks with visible brown coloration at the bruises
- Overgrown or stunted upper or lower beak

Causes

- Malnutrition, usually a deficiency in Biotin and calcium
- Possible Liver Damage
- Exposure to toxins and chemicals
- Infection and Injuries
- Applying too much pressure while hand feeding chicks

Treatment

- Providing dietary supplements in case of malnutrition
- Removal of ticks and parasites
- Biopsy to check for secondary ailments
- Trimming of the beak

Feather and Skin Disorders

Domestic Fowl are susceptible to several infections of their skin because of their constant contact with water. The feathers and the wings might show some sure shot signs of an infection. There are specific symptoms that you can watch out for in such cases.

Symptoms

- Angel Wings where the feathers are turned upwards
- Constant Scratching and preening
- Bald patches in the plumes
- Wet Feathers
- Cysts and Abscesses on the skin
- Soreness and redness of the skin
- Cysts
- Slipped wings that have feathers growing outwards

Causes

- Too much protein intake, especially in case of slipped wings and angel wings
- Ecto parasites
- Ticks and Mites
- Reduced secretion of waterproofing oils by glands present in the skin. This might be due to ruptured glands or malfunctioning glands
- Cysts and abscesses are usually caused by blocked glands
- Poor living and breeding conditions
- Infections and Injuries

Treatment

- Reduced protein intake
- Providing a balanced meal with recommended pellets and wheat

- Recommended powders or medication to treat parasites, ticks and mites
- Medicated feed to resolve issues pertaining to glands
- Maintaining a healthy and sanitary environment for the birds

Lameness in Chickens

A common problem that is found in chickens is lameness. They might have difficulty in walking and sometimes, just standing up. Since chickens are highly dependent on their limbs for locomotion, you must ensure that you take proper care to treat lameness or other problems with the legs.

Causes

- Sprained, Broken or injured joints
- Arthritis
- Cuts in the feet
- Damage to the muscles
- Pinched Nerves
- Hip Dislocation
- Splinters in the feet
- Bacterial Infections. A common bacterial infection in chickens is called bumblefoot. This leads to abscesses on the feet that make it difficult for the bird to walk properly.
- Inflammation of the tendons
- Damage to the Kidney
- Aging

Treatment

- Examine the legs and feet for cuts and splinters
- Check for abscesses at the bottom of the foot
- Provide the right diet, especially for growers
- Calcium and vitamin supplements
- Corrective dressing and casts in case of injuries

Note: Cover of all the wires and mesh in the coop where the legs might get caught and be injured.

Predatory Attack

While most predatory attacks are likely to end badly for your chicken, some chickens do survive such encounters. These episodes have three different problems that must be overcome for the chicken to survive.

Initially, the chicken must survive the attack. Chickens may be killed from broken necks, damaged organs, profuse bleeding (which can occur internally) or simply from the shock of the attack. Once they have survived this, the chicken will need your help to address any significant wounds.

Wash your chicken with a veterinary-approved wound wash or, if none is available, clean water. If there are any major lacerations, obviously broken bones or similar symptoms, you must take your chicken to the veterinarian immediately. Once these wounds are treated, the chicken must survive the last threat from such encounters: infection.

During the healing process, it is important to keep the injured chicken in a quiet, calm and clean habitat. Follow your veterinarian's instructions regarding access to swimming water, the administration of medications and any other follow up care.

While attacks are stressful events, with luck and prompt action, you may be able to help your chicken survive the encounter.

Poisoning

While not a "traumatic event" by the strictest definition, poisoning should be handled in a similar manner. The symptoms of poisoning vary with the causative agent at work, and are often only determined after ruling out other possible problems.

One frequent cause of poisoning is moldy food. Many molds that grow on wet cereal grains can cause serious illness or death for birds that consume them. Alfatoxins are one of the most important types to prevent. Always ensure that your chicken's food stays dry to prevent it from molding. Never feed chickens any food that may contain mold; if there is any doubt in the status of a given food, discard it and replace it with fresh food.

Botulism can occur if your chickens have access to stagnant, warm water, which allows the anaerobic bacteria Clostridium botulinum to thrive. Botulism usually produces a limp paralysis of the neck, wings and legs. Chickens usually lapse into a coma and die within two days of contracting the disease.

Additionally, several chemicals can be very toxic to chickens. Lead and zinc both cause muscle weakness, weight loss and digestive problems. Chickens may ingest lead in the form of old paint chips, lead shot or lead fishermen's weights. Zinc often comes from galvanized metal tubs and fixtures.

Mercury, which is derived from a variety of sources, (including the fish that the chickens eat) also causes weakness. Mercury may stay inside the chicken's body (or inside the eggs they produce) for many months after ingestion.

Phosphorus, which is found in a number of rodent poisons, matches and fireworks, can be especially deadly. While chickens sometimes exhibit weakness or depression upon ingesting phosphorus, they may also experience very sudden death, in which no symptoms occur.

Even relatively benign chemicals, such as salt, can cause health problems if ingested in large quantities. Salt used to de-ice roads often ends up at the bottom of the watershed – such as your chicken's pond. If enough is ingested, chickens may experience convulsions, kidney failure or even death.

Arsenic is another potentially dangerous chemical that your chickens may come into contact with. Used in a variety of poisons, arsenic is also present in some treated lumber. However, if the lumber has dried completely, it will not leach into the environment and harm your chickens. Chickens that eat arsenic show signs of nervousness, and they often die.

Carbon monoxide is an odorless, colorless gas that is often created by heating units. Always be sure that your chickens' shelter is well ventilated if you use a heating device. Carbon monoxide can cause very rapid death in most animals, including chickens.

This chapter discusses some of the most common health issues that chicken owners need to deal with. However, if you think that there are other symptoms that your chicken might be exhibiting, make sure you take him to a water fowl expert at the earliest. Never neglect even the slightest abnormality in the health of your chicken.

The other thing to remember is that you must never provide home remedies and medicines for pets. In case of chickens and poultry you must be additionally cautious as they may have infections that affect our health, too. Make sure you take your chicken for routine checkups to keep him in the pink of his health. In case you are negligent you will not only put your health at risk but will also have to shell out tones of money. Remember, taking care of the health of your chicken is expensive, as you require the services of specialized waterfowl vets. So the best thing to do is to keep your chickens healthy by providing them with a clean and healthy environment to live in.

5. Finding a Good Chicken Veterinarian

Unfortunately, the veterinarian you take your dog or cat to may not be qualified to treat your chickens. Fortunately, finding a veterinarian who specializes in farm animals or birds is not as hard to find as it was years ago.

To find a veterinarian, begin by asking the breeder, retailer or individual from whom you purchased the birds. Often, they will have a relationship with a veterinarian accustomed to caring for waterfowl. If that does not work, you can ask other chicken hobbyists in your area.

If none of these strategies allows you to locate a vet, search the Internet and local phone listings. If possible, search for reviews of the veterinarian before visiting him or her.

Remember that chickens are not dogs or cats, and a trip to the veterinarian can be an especially stressful event. Therefore, a veterinarian that makes house calls is especially helpful. However, your chickens may require hospitalization or surgery to remedy some illnesses, so it is important the veterinarian has access to a place suitable for such procedures.

Always locate and meet with your veterinarian soon after acquiring your flock. This way, you can become acquainted with the vet if you are not already, and your vet can give your chickens a preliminary physical to ensure they are healthy.

One of the other reasons to visit your veterinarian immediately after acquiring your chickens is to prevent the spread of any diseases they have to their new environment.

For example, if your newly purchased chickens have an illness, and you take them directly from the breeder to your garden, they may spread the disease throughout their enclosure.

Later, when you take them to the veterinarian and have them treated, you must then take them back to their enclosure, where they will become re-infected, thus necessitating further treatment. Additionally, you will be forced to clean the entire enclosure – including the water reservoir – from top to bottom.

Therefore, if at all possible, take the chickens directly from the place you acquire them to the veterinarian's office.

Many chicken breeders will determine the gender of the chickens for you, if this is not possible, your veterinarian should be able to determine the gender of the birds for you.

6. Guidelines to Help Prevent Disease

It is impossible to eliminate the potential for disease transmission. However, by following these three guidelines, you can greatly reduce the risks to your pets, and give them a better chance at living long, healthy lives:

- Minimize the stress on your chickens, so that their immune systems operate at peak efficiency.
- Do not let your chickens socialize. Keep your Chickens away from all other waterfowl.
- Immunize the chickens against as many diseases as possible.

By examining the ways in which different diseases can infect chickens, the reasons for these three guidelines are clear.

In broad terms, some infectious agents are ubiquitous, and only cause problems when they overwhelm an animal's immune system. This is most likely to occur in stressed animals that do not have access to proper housing, or are fed improper diets. Coccidiosis is one example of this type of pathogen. It infects most chickens, but usually only causes symptoms when a particularly lethal strain is ingested, or when the birds ingest large quantities of the sporulated oocysts (the infectious particles for these parasitic protozoans) (Larry R. McDougald, 2012).

Accordingly, it is important to provide your chicken with a clean habitat, feed it the most nutritious diet possible, and ensure that they are protected from inclement weather and temperature extremes, to avoid these types of pathogens, and the illnesses they cause.

Other infectious agents must pass from one host to another, and are not likely to infect chickens that do not come into contact with other chickens. For example, a chicken housed singly for the entirety of his life, who does not share water or space with other chickens, is unlikely to develop viral enteritis. However, a chicken only needs to sip infected water once to become infected, and ultimately die. Your flock will undoubtedly exchange germs amongst themselves, so you must effectively quarantine your flock. Try to purchase chickens from the same breeder or retailer, and avoid adding other members to the flock at a later time.

Take care to prevent wild chickens from sharing a pond with your flock. Additionally, be careful when visiting other places with chickens; a frequent way diseases are spread is via dirt particles that cling to people's shoes or clothing. Ensure that visitors have not recently been around other chickens.

Therefore, as explained in the first two guidelines, you should provide your chickens with the very best care possible, to ensure that your chickens' immune system is working as well as it can and that they do not share water, space or the company of other chickens.

Immunization is the process of injecting a dead, weakened or sub-infectious quantity of a virus into a potential host before it gets sick. When this occurs, the chickens' immune systems learn to fight off this virus, while not being at risk of becoming sick. This way, when the chickens eventually encounter the live virus, their immune systems defeat it, keeping them from getting sick.

Some vaccines provide lifetime immunity, while others must be given repeatedly to remain effective. Vaccines exist for chicken viral hepatitis, chicken viral enteritis and Riemerella anatipestifer infections, and others are under development (Major Viral Diseases of Waterfowl and Their Control, 2011).

By following these three guidelines, you are likely to reduce the chances of illness in your flock significantly.

Emergency and First Aid

If you notice injuries or sudden health problems in your chicken, choking for instance, you must be able to provide them with first aid. A well-equipped first aid kit is the first step towards ensuring immediate help for your birds. The must haves in your First Aid Kit are:

- Tweezers: Broken blood feathers are a common problem in chickens. If these feathers break or get damaged, they will bleed profusely. So it is recommended that you pluck them out gently using tweezers.

- Blood Coagulant: Injuries or breaking of blood feathers might cause profuse bleeding. It is good to have a blood coagulant to help take care of this issue.

- Bag Balm: This is a petroleum based product that can be used to soothe wounds and sores.

- Eye Ointment: When chickens get into fights, they are most often prone to eye injuries. Having an antibacterial eye ointment can prevent severe infections.

- Syringes or droppers: In some conditions like sour crop, you might have to drop water or oil directly into the throat of the chicken. Syringes and droppers can be used for this. They are also handy when you have to give your chicken oral medication.

- Rubber gloves: Handling chickens with injuries puts you at the risk of infections. Using rubber gloves will keep you safe.

Now that you have all the information you need on healthcare of Chickens, you can rest assured that you will be able to maintain your flocks well.

Conclusion

Now that you are equipped with all the information that you need with respect to the Buff Orpington Chickens, I am sure that you will make a great owner. It is a lot of work to keep chickens at home. While that may sound intimidating, if you are unable to match all the requirements and needs of your birds, you will only compromise on their health and well-being. To conclude, I would like to remind you that a chicken is a big financial commitment.

Here is a breakdown of the approximate costs of keeping a Buff Orpington Chicken:

- Coop: $500 to $1000 or £200 to £400
- Egg Incubators: $40 to $50 or £20 to £25
- Feed: $7 to $10 or £5 to £10 for a 20 pound bag
- Feeder: $3 to $10 or £5 to £10
- Waterer: $3 to $20 or £5 to £10
- Nesting box: $20 or £10
- Heater: $40 or £20
- Annual Vet cost: $150 to $1000 or £80 to £450

Once you are sure of making this commitment, you can convert your home into a great place for your Buff Orpington Chickens.

I hope this book answers all your questions about having Buff Orpington Chickens.

Published by IMB Publishing 2014

www.ingramcontent.com/pod-product-compliance
Lightning Source LLC
Chambersburg PA
CBHW072013040426
42447CB00009B/1612